AF262973

Praise for *In the Company of Nature*

'Several books argue for making business more sustainable, less destructive of the environment, and many of them tell us how to do so. Much rarer to find a practitioner who recognises that what we call the environment is simply, and gloriously, the life of the planet, of which we're an integral part. Once you say yes to that instinctive truth, you also realise that the regenerative capacity of natural systems, not mitigation of harm, becomes the precondition of sustainability. Now, this might inspire and comfort those in a classroom setting, but it comes with a dash of terror for those in business who make, transport and sell things in the world as it is. Frieda Gormley, in her wonderfully written new book, *In the Company of Nature*, never loses sight of the North Star for regenerative practices that also help define and inform her business decisions (Mother Nature has a representative serving on the board). Her story of her own journey of discovery and how it changed her life, her business and her relations with all her stakeholders, from suppliers to employees to investors, provides useful lessons and insights for the similarly inclined.'

VINCENT STANLEY, director of philosophy, Patagonia;
co-author of *The Future of the Responsible Company*

'Frieda obviously has a deep intuitive love and respect for Nature, and that comes through so strongly in this book. It is written so beautifully that it is extremely hard to put down, but it is also a blueprint for future businesses, ones that repay their debt to Nature and consider their people and purpose to be as important as profit. *In the Company of Nature* is a fascinating case study of an incredible journey, and Frieda is indomitable in her quest to ensure that Nature is rewarded for Her part in our lives.'

JANE SHEPHERDSON CBE, chair of My Wardrobe HQ

'A memoir and manifesto of the utmost delicacy – it is an ode to Nature.'

SIR PARTHA DASGUPTA GBE FBA FRS, Frank Ramsey
professor emeritus of economics, University of Cambridge

'This is the story of a modern business rooted in timeless values: compassion, creativity and responsibility to the world around us. Frieda Gormley's journey reminds us that the most powerful innovation comes when a company sees itself not above society but within it – deeply connected to people, planet and possibility.'

MARY PORTAS OBE

'House of Hackney has a marvellous mission: to transform the world of business. To make a shift from seeing Nature simply as a resource for financial growth to seeing Nature as life itself. This inspiring book makes a compelling case to see Nature not as a commodity but as a community, and it tells the heartwarming story of Frieda Gormley's business. Frieda is not just dreaming about some abstract ideals; she has the courage of her convictions to make her inspiring vision reality – even appointing Nature as a board member! A rare example. Every businessperson should read this book.'

SATISH KUMAR, founder of Schumacher College

'At a time when the old order is melting away before our eyes, we must heal ourselves, our communities, our businesses, our politics and, ultimately, Earth itself. I deeply admire what Frieda Gormley and her team are doing at House of Hackney – and highly recommend this account of how it all came together.'

JOHN ELKINGTON, author of *Tickling Sharks: How We Sold Business on Sustainability*

'This story of a wonderful company, and the curious minds that built it, doesn't have to make the case for Nature. They listened closely, and Nature made the case for itself. Drink it all in; let these pioneers help you to listen.'

KRESSE WESLING CBE, co-founder of Elvis & Kresse

'Frieda Gormley has written a moving autobiography and postmodern business book that should be compulsory reading for all those searching for an insight into a new vision of capitalism, where spiritual awareness, entrepreneurism and righteous anger at the betrayal of a great concept by unfettered greed come blinking into a hoped-for New Dawn. A love letter to being alive, yet underneath the fluffy stuff, a muscular champion for business, community and planetary health.'

Sir Tim Smit, co-founder of The Lost Gardens
of Heligan and the Eden Project

'Frieda Gormley is a pioneer, a force of Nature, and this is a simply brilliant book. An unlikely mix of autobiography, governance manual and campaign handbook, it demonstrates clearly how small businesses committed to Nature and future generations can become a collective force that heals through legally redefining their purpose and mission. Once named Young Entrepreneur of Ireland, Frieda brings imagination and intelligence to the idea of rewriting the role of business to protect what we love, so you can do it too. As she says herself, "We don't need to have it all figured out. We just need to begin. To start where we are. To follow what feels alive. To tend to what feels true." So, start here. Read this book and be inspired to act.'

Jane Davidson, author of *#futuregen*

'Reinventing our relationship with Nature is the key issue of the twenty-first century, and every business will eventually have to grapple with it. What better way to begin that journey than to read the story of a company that has trailblazed a path to a better economic model, one which makes Nature intrinsic to its business. In this book, Frieda and House of Hackney are unafraid to ask the questions we all really need to be answering.'

Paul Powlesland, river guardian; barrister;
founder of Lawyers for Nature

'Frieda blends dreams, myth, hard science and business common sense to bring us this riveting story about House of Hackney. Actually, it's more than just a story about one company; it's a story of many small and medium businesses and their founders who strive to create businesses that are a force for good – a force for restoration and regeneration.

'By telling it so vividly, Frieda is framing a blueprint (or greenprint as she calls it, because this story is not meant to be unique) for many others to be equally audacious and unapologetic about doing the right thing and move wholeheartedly from extraction to regeneration.'

Anuradha Chugh, co-chair of B Lab UK

'While House of Hackney may sell luxury products, its approach to Nature is a necessity. Frieda Gormley's *In the Company of Nature* is a compelling blend of narrative, provocation and greenprint. She explains how businesses must view Nature not as a resource to be exploited nor a risk to be avoided, but rather as a living system that partners with all we do. We can all benefit by giving Nature a voice – and listening to it.'

PETER TUFANO, professor, Harvard Business School;
former dean, Saïd Business School, University of Oxford

'Building a truly regenerative business in a degenerative economy is an act of integrity. *In the Company of Nature* reveals the inspiring story about a business born of a young couple's unrequited love for "home-making". A clear vision, a belief in intuition, and uncommon courage and grit earn the young House of Hackney and its founders the gift we all yearn for in these troubled times: a purpose worthy of a life, and a "coming home" to the beauty and serenity of all life.'

JOHN FULLERTON, founder of the Capital Institute;
author of *Regenerative Economics*

'*In the Company of Nature* is a beautiful and touching book. Frieda lets the reader share in her personal and professional journey – the ongoing sense-making of a business leader exploring in depth what it means to *be* Nature and to do what life does best: create conditions for life to thrive. Navigating the paradoxes of our time, this personal story of the co-creation of a successful luxury brand with that intention in mind offers insights, inspiration and encouragement to align with life's regenerative impulse. Enjoy the read!'

DANIEL WAHL, author of *Designing Regenerative Cultures*

In the Company of Nature

REGENERATING BUSINESS, COMMUNITY AND THE LIVING WORLD

Frieda Gormley

Chelsea Green Publishing
White River Junction, Vermont
London, UK

First published in 2026 by Chelsea Green Publishing | PO Box 4529 |
White River Junction, VT 05001 | West Wing, Somerset House, Strand |
London, WC2R 1LA, UK | www.chelseagreen.com
A Division of Rizzoli International Publications, Inc. | 49 West 27th Street |
New York, NY 10001 | www.rizzoliusa.com

Copyright © 2026 by Frieda Gormley.
All rights reserved.

No part of this book may be transmitted or reproduced in any form by any means
without permission in writing from the publisher.

Publisher: Charles Miers
Deputy Publisher: Matthew Derr
Commissioning Editor: Muna Reyal
Project Manager: Susan Pegg
Copy Editor: Susan Pegg
Proofreader: Jacqui Lewis
Indexer: Lisa Footitt
Designer: Abrah Griggs

ISBN 978-1-64502-350-0 (hardcover) | ISBN 978-1-64502-388-3 (ebook) |
ISBN 978-2-64502-485-9 (audiobook)
Library of Congress Control Number: 2026002423 (print)
A CIP catalogue record for this book is available from the British Library.

Our Commitment to Green Publishing
Chelsea Green sees publishing as a tool for cultural change and ecological stewardship. We
strive to align our book manufacturing practices with our editorial mission and to reduce the
impact of our business enterprise in the environment. We print our books using vegetable-
based inks whenever possible. This book may cost slightly more because it was printed on
paper that contains recycled fiber, and we hope you'll agree that it's worth it. *In the Company of
Nature* was printed on paper supplied by Marquis that is made of recycled materials and other
controlled sources.

Authorized EU representative for product safety and compliance
Mondadori Libri S.p.A. | www.mondadori.it
via Gian Battista Vico 42 | Milan, Italy 20123

Printed in Canada.
10 9 8 7 6 5 4 3 2 1   26 27 28 29 30

For Javi and Lila – and those who come after.

CONTENTS

Irish Proverb

Fatherland

'We are the ones we've been waiting for.'
Attributed to the Hopi Elders

I too am just two generations removed from living with the land. My story of separation is likely much like yours. I am part of a generation that still holds a fragile thread that ties us to a time when we *were* connected to the land. My paternal grandmother, Bea, a smallholding farmer in the west of Ireland, lived with her hands in the soil every day. I don't think she would have used the word 'organic' for the pesticide-free potatoes, turnips and carrots that she grew to feed her family. Nor for the chickens that roamed the farmyard and the herd of cattle in the field below that provided the raw organic milk to make her children strong, but that is exactly what they were.

This small-scale farming, guided by the traditions of previous generations who had worked in rhythm with the land, was as much about nourishing her family as it was about earning a small income to support their modest lives. Through her farming rituals, Bea was continuing an ancient ancestral dance with the land that had been taking place across millennia. What she would not have known, but what science is now starting to acknowledge, is the alchemical connection that was activated through this primal exchange of body and earth. That the same bacteria that enrich the earth also live within us, forming flourishing ecosystems on our skin and in our gut. And the more we connect with the land, the more we have our fingers in the soil or the earth under our feet, the more diverse and resilient our microbiomes become. Crucial not just for our physical health but also our mental health, triggering as it does the release of the 'happy hormone', serotonin, that soothes the nervous system and lifts our mood. The fields, worked by my grandmother, did more than yield food; they were places of healing. She was tending to her soul as she tended to the soil.

As a child, I can remember how my grandmother spoke of the land and the weather as if they were animated, sentient forces, unpredictable and powerful. She wove her Catholic faith seamlessly with her awe of Nature's raw presence, offering prayers to saints and storms alike. In that liminal corner of the west of Ireland, time moved differently. New ideas arrived slowly and with hesitation as they took their time to embed themselves into the old ways of being.

Though the Catholic Church wielded immense influence, the spirit of the ancient Brehon laws still lingered in Ireland, woven so tightly into our cultural fabric that they remain part of our collective personality even today. These laws, which governed Ireland for over a thousand years, understood Nature not as a resource to be dominated but as a sacred, interconnected web of life, something science is now proving but that was innate and unquestioned by ancient cultures. The Brehon laws offered legal protections to rivers, forests and wildlife, honouring their intrinsic value and their role in sustaining all living things; a thousand years before the Rights of Nature movement arrived to remind us of the inherent rights of all life on Earth. Under Brehon law, harming the land or animals was not merely a personal or spiritual offence but a legal one, carrying fines or reparations to restore balance. This ancient code reflected a worldview in which humans were participants in, and not masters over, the natural world.

Like his father before him, and even *his* father before that, my grandfather, Michael, worked as head carpenter for the 'Big House', the seat of the local landed gentry. Each day on his walk to work, he passed through the vast fir woods where the estate's trees were felled for timber and later transformed into beams, doors and furniture by his skilled hands. Unknown to him, the forest was healing him. The trees released phytoncides – natural plant chemicals that reduced any stress and supported his immunity. Those woods were offering not just timber but medicine, too. Like my grandmother a few miles down the road with her hands in the earth, my grandad was participating in the ancient biological exchange between body and land that would keep them both in rude health and carried them into their late eighties and nineties. My grandparents lived with the land, in natural harmony with its rhythms, knowing when to sow and when to reap. They ate what the earth provided, the gifts of the seasons, Nature providing the nourishment their bodies required exactly when it was needed.

Community was a lifeline in this isolated landscape, where unforgiving weather and a dwindling population still haunted by the ravaging of the famine could make for a lonely existence. People worked the fields together, sang the *sean-nós* together, birthed new life and waked the dead together.

My father was the first to break the cycle. He left the fields behind for the bright lights of Boston, his bright mind begging to flee a life increasingly perceived as backward. And who could blame him? Dad was already three generations from the famine, but it was still casting its long shadow over the lands and communities it had decimated. Like the millions of Irish emigrants who had left before him, he set off on a path to America that would sever him from the roots that had nourished our family through the generations.

And so, we arrive at my generation.

We find ourselves in a time where we are completely separated from the land. It happened slowly, and then all at once. Progress arrived cloaked in promises with wealth as the key to happiness, as individualism replaced community and materialism replaced meaning. The economic story of extraction and consumption became the predominant narrative, and it has been since the Industrial Revolution. It promised endless growth and productivity as the North Star of purpose, focusing on how much profit could be squeezed from people and the earth alike. This so-called 'progress' pulled us indoors and into ourselves, confining us to walls and screens, and left us chasing insatiable satisfaction that dissolved as quickly as a fast-food meal. We are the first generation who spend more time on screens than looking into our children's eyes. We can just about recall what it was like to climb trees instead of chasing levels in online games. And the names of the oaks and the ashes and the giant horse chestnut, and how their leaves felt pressed into our little sweaty palms. We remember the time before our lives were called indoors.

At a cellular level, I can feel the disconnection from the land. My atoms and molecules still hum with the memory of living in rhythm with Nature. The further we have drifted away from our place within Nature, the more we have forgotten what it is like to feel whole. And this separation from our birthright of living in relationship with the natural world is costing us dearly. On the surface, it's a bleak picture. Our bodies are showing signs of this separation as it manifests itself in chronic stress, burnout, illness, loneliness and feeling deeply disconnected from community and from ourselves – literally dis-eased.

I still have fading memories of long 1980s summers spent outdoors, where the road was our playground, and of the freewheeling 90s, when adolescence unfolded in the real-life community of teenage tribes, not yet distorted by the relentless pressures of social media. This childhood gave me solid building blocks for foundational health and resilience. Those days spent outdoors with friends nurtured not only our bodies but also our spirit and it taught us how to thrive in relationships – with Nature, with each another and with ourselves.

As we moved indoors and lost touch with the natural world, as we experienced it less, we also lost our impulse to protect it. Because we protect what we are in a relationship with. We protect what we love.

And yet, we are living in times of profound transformation. The old stories of unchecked growth, extraction and exploitation are starting to crumble. In their place, new stories are beginning to emerge. Stories of community, of collaboration and connection. Stories that honour all life on Earth, not as resources to be used but as kin to be respected. These are stories that don't just soothe us but reorient us. They reflect science. They echo what Indigenous cultures have long known: that we are not separate from Earth but made of Her. That we breathe with the trees. That we are not just visitors here but that we *are* Nature, remembering and defending herself. And that it is our birthright to live that way. To live in connection with Nature. To work in harmony with Earth's cycles. To honour our circadian rhythms – those ancient biological clocks that govern our bodies and that no amount of tech innovation is going to change. To raise children who know the names of trees, the calls of birds, the feeling of soil between their fingers, grounding them in the biodiversity that sustains all life. Not just because of the awesome beauty but because it is our life force. And as we do, so we pass on more than knowledge. We pass on resilience, reverence and an ancestral blueprint for thriving in balance with the living world.

As the last generation with even a faint memory of what it was like to live in something akin to a tribe, to have adventures outside, to belong to a close-knit community, ours is a unique calling. In these transitional times where the old paradigms collapse, we stand at the crossroads of ancestral wisdom and emerging new ways with a rising remembering.

As the Hopi Elders prophesised, 'We are the ones we've been waiting for.'

Our purpose is to be the keepers of memory, the midwives of transition, as we help birth a new way of life that honours the sacred interconnectedness of all things. But to even open the door, we must first forge the key – one shaped for the unlocking of a new yet ancient way of being and doing that honours all life. In truth, it is less an invention than a remembrance.

We have to honour the land as our grandparents knew it – fuller, wilder, more alive than even our own childhoods – and to carry that memory as a compass for our work. We do this not just for ourselves but for those who come after us: for the future generations who deserve to inherit a world with that same level of beauty and abundance that is their birthright.

We are the bridge generation – walking with the memory of the past and the possibility of the future as we step into the work of restoration.

CHAPTER 1

On Purpose

'The human is less a being on the earth or in the universe than a dimension of the earth and indeed of the universe itself.'

Thomas Berry, *The Dream of the Earth*

We have lungs that mirror the branching of trees.

Our thumbprints echo the circles of age on an ancient tree stump.

Our veins resemble the tributaries of a river and the veins of a leaf.

Our circadian rhythms follow the waxing and waning of our days and the seasons.

We are made from the same material and are bound by the same cycles as every other form of life.

We are not separate but an expression of Nature herself.

Which means we too must have a purpose, a role to play, even if we have strayed from it.

What's my purpose? What am I here for?

I've thought long and hard about our human purpose on Earth and have had some big conversations about this question. Every other species contributes effortlessly, intuitively and perfectly to create the equilibrium of life. From the earthworm who turns fertile soil to support life beneath the ground to the beaver who slows the rivers, birthing rich wetlands that foster biodiversity, to the bee whose pollination sustains entire food chains. To the fungi as they decompose fallen matter, returning it to the soil and nourishing the forest floor, ready for the earthworm to play his part in the cycle all over again. Each organism plays a vital, irreplaceable role in the great pattern of the whole.

But we appear to be the only species that takes without giving back and the only one that generates waste no other organism can metabolise. Even in our most basic exchange with Nature, when we are gifted our life force of oxygen by the trees, we return carbon dioxide in excess, exhaling what Earth cannot absorb quickly enough. We pave over habitats, poison waterways, pollute the air and destabilise the climate as we disrupt the delicate feedback loops that countless other species strive to maintain with their purposeful contributions. Where they work in service of the whole, our aim is usually to extract, forgetting that we are a part of – and not apart from – the very system that sustains us.

We selfishly prioritise personal gain over collective wellbeing as we act individually in a system that depends on relationships and as we make decisions that benefit the now at the expense of the future. We are unbelievably short-sighted in a world that requires our deep-time vision. And perhaps the most sobering truth of all is that if humans were to vanish tomorrow, Nature would bounce back and recover. Forests would regrow. Air and water would purify. But if, in contrast, the bees disappeared, or the fungi, or the coral reefs, or the wolves, the ripple effects would be seismic as ecosystems unravelled – collapsing food webs, disrupting the structures that keep life sustained, endangering countless lifeforms, ourselves included.

Yet the very fact that we can reflect on this, that we ask these deep questions at all, reveals a deeper truth. Some say we are Nature made conscious – a thought that invites both humility and responsibility.

Sometimes I find myself awestruck by the sheer improbability of it all: that for all we currently know, life, in all its splendour and complexity, may have only happened here on Earth. That across the vast silence of the universe, this blue-green planet may be the single flicker of consciousness. If that's true, then the weight of our responsibility is almost unbearable. It makes me want to shout our privilege of existence from rooftops while also wanting to shake people into realising that we could destroy, in a few short centuries, the only instance of life the cosmos has ever known. It is a thought that is both humbling and mind-blowing. Because if we truly are Nature made conscious, then our role is not to dominate life but to safeguard it and ensure that this absolute miracle of life endures.

In many ways, it's clear that humanity today stands at the threshold of adulthood. As I raise teenagers, I see the parallels everywhere. Like them, as a species we are brimming with raw intelligence and immense creativity, yet we push limits, seek identity and ignore consequences. We resist restraint, ignore the wisdom of elders and largely assume someone else will clean up the mess we've made.

On the evolutionary timeline, *Homo sapiens*, at only about 300,000 years old, is still remarkably young, a blink in life on Earth's 3.7-billion-year history. No wonder we find ourselves grappling with the consequences of our young power. But adolescence is only a phase – a messy, necessary stage on the way towards maturity. And like the human teenagers that we are, we take longer to mature than almost any other species on Earth. In the natural world, most animals gain independence shortly after birth. But humans stay close to their parents – and their wider kinship networks – for years, sometimes decades. We are biologically wired to require guidance, learning and care over a prolonged period.

So, it doesn't seem to be a coincidence that we find ourselves at this watershed moment of a collective global rite of passage manifesting as a planetary crisis, that calls us to learn the wisdom of what it means to be in right relationship with power, freedom and responsibility. And how we need to wield these powers in service of life. Like any teenager standing on the cusp of adulthood, we need the guidance, mentorship and care of our elders to mature into conscious, responsible participants in life.

Perhaps this threshold we find ourselves at – in this liminal space between collapse and emergence – isn't about inventing something entirely new but about remembering what has always lived within us and restoring our purpose by reclaiming our place in Nature.

The more I've studied Nature's beauty to inspire our designs at House of Hackney, the company I co-founded with my husband, Javvy, and the deeper I go beneath Her sublime patterns and colours, the more I humbly arrive at the truth of Nature's exquisitely intelligent, self-organising systems. That there is a reason for every species to exist.

In Nature, there are no mistakes as we understand them. Nature evolves, reacts, experiments, self-corrects. Every organism, every function, every relationship is part of a larger, dynamic awesome whole, far more than the sum of its parts; and then some. There is no waste in Nature. The carbon exhaled by animals becomes the breath of plants. Even a fallen tree isn't the end of life but the beginning again of the cycle of regeneration as a nutritious habitat for fungi, insects and new growth. Every species, from microbes to whales, plays a part in the intricate, ever-evolving whole.

And we are no exception. We are Nature expressed in human form, composed of the same biological materials as every other organism on Earth. So, surely, we must serve a purpose. We, too, must have a role within the greater pattern of life. In the great unfolding of evolution, we've come to understand that even disruptions can serve a function. Forest fires clear dead wood to make way for new growth. Floods reshape landscapes. Predators create balance.

Mother Nature has bestowed on us a set of unique gifts that, if used wisely, may guide us back to our deeper purpose – not merely as participants in the system but as conscious stewards of it. We carry the gift of moral imagination: the capacity to imagine not just what *is* but what *could* be, empowering us to make choices not just based on instinct or ease or proximity but grounded in values and responsibility, even when the outcome may not be seen in our lifetime. Coupled with this is our ability to plan for the long term, not merely for seasons or cycles but across generations.

We are creatures of narrative, with a capacity for not just telling stories but of rewriting them. We are uniquely able to carry knowledge, art, wisdom and memory through language and across time. We don't just shape individual behaviour, we shape collective worldviews, values and moral codes. And perhaps most remarkably, we hold the gift of agency in restoration.

It is clear to me that Mother Nature endowed us with these gifts not just for survival but for intergenerational stewardship, entrusting to us the power of story, memory, and the inherent human capacity to imagine and build a better world. I really believe that we are the generation called to bridge the two worlds we find ourselves straddling – a world built on separation and a world rooted in reconnection.

It's almost as though evolution has taken a bold leap, in creating a species that doesn't just respond to change but can also consciously direct life. As Earth system science shows, human activity today is shaping the planet on a scale once reserved for glaciers, volcanoes and asteroids. We are living in an epoch some scientists call the Anthropocene – a new geological era defined by our human impact on climate, biodiversity, oceans and soil. In simple terms, it means we've unwittingly become our own force of Nature.

From a scientific perspective, we are placed in the role of a keystone species, as organisms whose presence have an outsized influence on the ecosystems around them.

And in that lies both our greatest responsibility and our greatest hope.

So, along this path of questioning and reckoning, I came to realise that our existence isn't actually random and that humanity, like every other species, has its own specific role to play in the great story of life. This epiphany catalysed a feeling in me that I needed to rise to meet my own purpose, to contribute to our collective one, in this urgent and emergent moment on Earth that we have been born into.

In the Global North, we're often taught that finding one's purpose is the zenith of self-actualisation: a singular, personal quest often as elusive as the end of the rainbow. However, I've come to realise that the purpose isn't solely an individual endeavour but a communal one. In Nature, no being seeks its purpose, it simply expresses it, by fulfilling its role in the larger system. I'm pretty sure that the bee does not ponder its pollination. That the fungi do not contemplate their decomposition. Purpose is expressed through participation – through being in the right relationship with the greater whole. And so, it must be for us.

It is about aligning our unique gifts with the needs of the world. It does not announce itself with grand declarations but reveals itself in moments of deep flow and aliveness – like a river running clear along its natural course. Purpose, like life itself, tends to emerge and flourish under the right conditions, when we are in the right relationship: with ourselves, with our environment, with the people around us.

As a young child, a deep shyness and a porous sensitivity drove me inwards, where I created worlds within worlds, building stories and painting scenes that never quite matched the sheer vividness of my dreams. I'd vanish for hours into those imagined worlds, painting, making, building kingdoms in my garden, heart pounding with the deep trance of creation, oblivious to anything else but the force of creating pulsing through me. It seems to me now that I was trying to counteract the weight of the outer world by concocting otherworldly inner landscapes. With school came an academic capability that led me down a different path, ultimately speaking more to my head than to my heart. And as those early flames of creativity diminished and then were extinguished, I spent the best part of a decade feeling rudderless, burned out from chasing a version of life that didn't quite fit, unsure where my kinetic spark had gone.

But purpose has its own pace. And when the right conditions returned, so did the first flickers. In my mid-twenties, something began to stir again, and I started to feel the pulse of that earlier life force again – that heady feeling of a head and soul alignment.

The shift wasn't immediate but was fostered. I had stepped onto a career path that started to resonate with my abilities and instincts. I bought my first home and fell in love with the creative process of building my own worlds within those walls. Then, I got a new job and moved to London. There, the right conditions were at play – space, inspiration, creativity, community.

Meeting Javvy was like adding the bricks to something already solid. Just as the gift of unconditional love from our parents helps us flourish, this was unconditional love in romantic form, where my true, authentic self, flaws and all, was loved to its core. And that love was fully reciprocated, creating the conditions to activate not just my personal flourishing but the beginning of something we would grow together; building on those foundational bricks to create our collective purpose, our House. That initial seed would eventually become House of Hackney – an interiors brand born in our home in East London from our shared love of Nature's designs. But as the House grew, and as we observed our design muses, the flowers and the trees, even closer, so did the metaphorical garden we were planting. Mother Nature evolved from being our wellspring of creativity to becoming our greatest teacher. What started as a design brand became the framework for something far greater: a journey into how beauty, creativity and business itself might serve life, with Nature as its core.

House of Hackney was born as an antidote to the extractive models we had worked in. An attempt to reweave business back into its right relationship with people, place and planet. Of course, we needed to make a living, but our motivations were never purely financial; we didn't set it up to chase unicorn status or fast exits, to build quickly and flog it – a route that we could have taken. We simply wanted to create beautiful products that we couldn't find, and a type of culture that seemed even scarcer – a company where creativity could flourish, where relationships could be nourished and where Nature, our design muse, could be cherished.

From the beginning we were led by our hearts, but we certainly weren't setting out to birth a new model. The word *regenerative* would only come to us later, naming a way of working that doesn't just sustain, but restores and enriches life, giving back more than we take and opening the possibility that business might become a force that heals rather than only harms. Nor did we expect Mother Nature to become our compass on the journey. But after those first precarious start-up years, once our heads rose above water and the business steadied, the current shifted. With privilege came responsibility, and with knowledge and an ever-deepening awe of the natural world came a tug on our conscience. A call to step up, followed by an ambition to see if we could restore more than we took. Could we use our company not just as a business but as an incubator; a testbed for models that work with ecosystems, not against them? Looking back, like all living things, our journey emerged and gently flourished when the right conditions were in place, when we came into the right relationships: with ourselves, with our environment and with the people around us.

These are the big questions that are beginning to shape our path. The journey of creating a company that fulfils its reason for being, its purpose of being in service to and inspired by the greatest model and wisest mentor we could ask for: Mother Nature.

Our own path towards creating a purposeful business, much like the discovery and journey of my personal one, didn't reveal itself through grand declarations but through the quiet nudges that steered us onto the right track. But, over time, the reveal came through listening to our hearts, attuning to what was happening around us and, more than anything, tuning into Nature herself.

We learn daily, and as we know better, we need to apply better. It continues to be a bare-knuckle ride where we are (and have been flung) outside all comfort zones, but it leaves us feeling at our most alive, most aligned in our collective purpose, most in our flow. Not pushing against life but pulsing with it. We've had to get comfortable with the uncomfortable. We've become resilient with the unknown. But the upsides and returns – across the traditional and more holistic metrics of business success – are showing signs of what we always expected to be true. That a business designed to honour its place in Nature is smart business.

CHAPTER 2

The Business of Becoming

'All flourishing is mutual.'

Robin Wall Kimmerer, *The Serviceberry*

I'll admit I've had moments of deep self-doubt. House of Hackney is just one business, on the cusp of moving from small to medium-sized, and standing on the threshold of moving from a conventional model to a more regenerative one. A little voice on my shoulder would often whisper, 'It's not big enough. It's not established enough to have any impact.'

That voice echoes a wider story that many of us have internalised – that real influence belongs to the giants, the experts, the institutions. But I've learned to quieten that narrative and return to my core belief – and our mission – that change doesn't just come from the top down but often begins from the ground up.

The opportunity for business to help solve some of the greatest crises of our time is immense. Business is one of the most powerful levers we have – to model change, to demonstrate new ways of being and doing that honour all life, and to use the influence of brand to shift the cultural narrative.

We often feel beholden to big corporations – to the giants who shape markets, lobby governments and extract value at the expense of life. But there's a fact that always staggers me: 99 per cent of businesses in both the UK and the US are SMEs (small and medium-sized enterprises), which translates to a collective contribution of £2.75 trillion to private sector revenue in the UK and $13.3 trillion in the US. This means that most of the business world is made up of people like us – humans working in smaller, more adaptable ecosystems with the potential to lead real, regenerative change from the ground up. These businesses aren't the fringe players they are taken for. Instead, SMEs make up the overwhelming majority of businesses, employing nearly half the workforce and contributing significantly to national productivity. Imagine if we came together as SMEs and harnessed that collective power for change.

Whether we're founders, employees, customers or the future generation of workers, the opportunity to become a vital part of the solutions we need is immense – **especially** when it comes to restoring Nature, repairing systems and reimagining business as a force for regeneration. If we can learn from the blueprint of life that Nature so generously provides, SMEs could become one of the most powerful vehicles for change in our time.

Just as you'd never think, simply by looking at it, that a seed holds the blueprint for an entire forest, I have to trust that what we're nurturing now at House of Hackney contains the potential for something more far-reaching than what can yet be seen. From this size and this place, we are an agile incubator of new possibilities – not in spite of our scale but because of it. With a team of around fifty people, we are pretty well-positioned to cultivate, test, learn and share – to explore new ways of working and being that might resonate not just with other SMEs but with anyone, at any level, who is part of an organisation.

Being small allows us the adaptability to experiment, the intimacy to remain connected and the freedom to do things differently. Small *is* beautiful. We're exploring how a company might become more than just a vehicle for profit: how it might become a force for regeneration, a culture of care, a participant in the restoration of life. In many ways, we are a living lab – testing ideas in real time, learning through doing, and sharing what works (and what doesn't) with others walking a similar path. But don't be mistaken – this is not a linear journey. And like Nature herself, we are growing in cycles, not straight lines, evolving at the pace that's right for us without forcing it, at the perfect time we're meant to. Our House of Hackney journey, like any business and life itself, has not been straightforward. We've faced setbacks, rejections and unknowns. But in those moments of disruption, we've also found unexpected clarity. Closed doors have become invitations to new directions. Life, it seems, often has better timing, and holds ideas far greater than the ones we map for ourselves. We are not on a journey to some fixed 'there' but learning to walk with what unfolds.

This book is a personal story – my own search for meaning through the vehicle of business. But more than that, it's our collective story: a shared longing to return to our rightful place in the living world. It's a journey without a final destination. A continual enquiry. A spiral path that brings us back to what we've always known but are just beginning to remember. Not above it, not separate from it, but woven into it as threads in the great tapestry of life. Because like Nature, our true purpose is relational – to give more than we take, to tend to the soil beneath us and to leave the world richer for having passed through it. This is not a journey we walk alone. It's a collective movement towards reconnection, towards regeneration, towards remembering.

———

Growing up, I never really thought about the purpose of business. In my local village, they were simply the places where we bought our sweets, shopped for our food, rented our videos, booked our holidays and drank our pints. To my young eyes, it was clear they served our community's needs. There was an inherent reciprocity where we supported our local businesses, and those businesses provided us with what we needed in return. These exchanges were as relational as they were transactional. Money and goods moved between hands, but so, also, did conversation, care and trust. The butcher, the baker, the bank teller, knew my parents' names and stories. The newsagent would slip me a few extra cola bottle penny sweets into the brown paper bag with a wink. There was an invisible current running beneath each sale: a web of relationships that stitched the community together.

But it wasn't until my twenties when I got my first proper job in a large high-street corporation, on a scale I'd never experienced before, that I began to see something different. For the first time, I became aware that business is not always reciprocal, and that the transaction can often be exploitative. That it can extract more than it needs – money, time, energy, people, Nature – all siphoned off for the benefit of a few, at the cost of everything else.

A company was once defined as a group of people who share bread, from the Latin *com* (together) and *panis* (bread). Not an entity designed to maximise profit but a community, bound by relationship, interdependence and mutual nourishment. Somewhere along the way, we lost that meaning. The rise of industrial capitalism turned companies into machines for extraction of labour, of natural resources and of meaning. The relational became transactional. The community became corporate. Purpose was flattened into profit, and success was measured only in scale and growth.

There are ideas so deeply woven into the fabric of our worldviews that we don't even realise they're constructs at all. To me, the economy was an example of this. I just assumed it was a fixed reality, a neutral system governed by logic, numbers and possibly even science. Perhaps it's because I didn't go to business school, although I imagine it's often taught that way. Either way, I accepted without much questioning that the economy was grounded in immutable laws. That a business had to be driven by profit. That success meant growth, scale and market dominance.

It wasn't until much later, when I found myself inside the system, witnessing its extractive practices firsthand, that I began to see how wrong I'd got it. That the economy isn't some law of Nature or an inevitable force of physics or biology but a totally human narrative – a story we've created. A system of ideas, structures, agreements and incentives that has taken us far from the original root of the word: *oikonomia*, the ancient Greek term for 'care of the household'. Its original intention wasn't to maximise markets or accumulate wealth for the few but to steward resources for the wellbeing of the whole. That origin story feels almost utopian now, so far have we drifted from it that we barely recognise the original meaning and intention.

Over the last few hundred years, instead of continuing with the ancient worldview rooted in relationship that held our way of life for millennia, we veered onto a different path as Western societies adopted a radically new way of seeing the world and reframed how humans saw themselves in relation to Nature. This shift began during the Enlightenment and the Industrial Revolution and changed philosophy, science and industry as constructs, creating stories that still underpin our economy, our institutions and our education systems today.

As we failed to recognise our economy's place as embedded within the living world, we started to treat it as a closed, mechanical system, where each part could be broken down, optimised and controlled, with its outcomes predicted in advance. In doing so, we turned away from the real laws of Nature – laws that show us that life is emergent, complex and deeply interconnected, and that the whole is always far greater than simply the sum of its parts. This mechanistic worldview became the operating system of the modern world. It became the blueprint for how we built organisations, trained leaders, evaluated progress and defined success.

Nowhere is this more visible than in the evolution of modern management. In the early twentieth century, Frederick Winslow Taylor developed what he called 'scientific management'. He believed businesses should function like machines, with workers treated as interchangeable parts to be measured, timed and optimised for output. 'In the past the man has been first; in the future the system must be first,' he wrote.* His ideas became the blueprint for corporate structure with its laser focus on performance metrics, KPIs (key performance indicators), siloed departments and the obsession with efficiency at all costs.

The roots of this mindset lie in what writer Charles Eisenstein calls the 'story of separation', which is the dominant narrative of modernity that imagines humans as apart from, rather than a part of, the living world – a theme also explored by thinkers like Joanna Macy and David Abram. I wasn't taught this story at school, nor were you. Or at least not in its entirety. We are taught the part about progress, industry and human ingenuity, but not the revelation of the greater losses along the way as our sense of kinship with the living world was severed.

Once I heard this story, and how it reduced humans and the wider living world into mechanical parts, I began to notice its combative

---

* Frederick Winslow Taylor, *The Principles of Scientific Management* (Harper & Brothers, 1911), 7.

language everywhere. We speak of 'target markets', 'hostile takeovers' and 'competitive advantage' as if business were a battlefield. But what we are forgetting is that businesses are actually living systems made up of biological beings that interact with Nature. And in living systems we know that fragmentation leads to weakness, not strength. Health emerges through relationship, integration and resilience. The principle we should be working from is not 'divide and conquer' but unite and flourish.

And when we see life as fragments to be conquered, we end up with measures of progress that mistake destruction for growth. We measure a country's success through GDP (gross domestic product) as if the relentless production of goods, regardless of whether they're weapons, fossil fuels or fast fashion, equates to national wellbeing. But GDP tells us nothing about the health of our ecosystems, the happiness and fulfilment of our people or the resilience of our communities. It counts the money spent cleaning up disasters as a measure of success, but not the value of preventing them. GDP grows when forests are cut down but it puts no value on them being alive. In clinging to GDP as a guiding metric, we've confused output with wellbeing, and it's driving all the wrong activity.

There are rare but radical exceptions. Instead of GDP, Bhutan famously measures gross national happiness, prioritising spiritual, social and ecological wellbeing over productivity. New Zealand, too, has begun integrating wellbeing indicators into its national budget, investing in mental health, child welfare and environmental restoration as measures of national success.

But for the rest of us, we value a successful business by profitability and EBITDA (earnings before interest, taxes, depreciation and amortisation) as if the bottom line alone tells us whether a company is truly thriving. But just like GDP, these financial metrics ignore what really matters. They don't tell us about *how* that profit was made, and *who* or *what* was harmed in the process, or whether the business is extinguishing more life than it supports. We confuse business output with health, and it ends up driving the same extractive mentality as we reward short-term gains over long-term health and growth at any cost.

This same distortion of value seeps into how we define intelligence. Just as we've come to confuse a social media following with worth, we've also come to equate speed and recall with wisdom. In a culture obsessed with ranking and measuring, we've reduced intelligence to standardised tests and academic performance, as if logic, speed and memory are the only valid forms of knowing. But in a world that is finally waking up to the richness of neurodiversity, that definition is quickly dating. We are remembering that intelligence also lives in intuition, emotional sensitivity, creativity and care – qualities that can't always be tested but are essential for life. And yet, because they don't always fit neatly into metrics, we continue to undervalue them.

We've forgotten the veritable truths that soil health underpins food security. That mental health shapes economic productivity. That social cohesion is what enables communities to weather crises. And that going to the root and creating ecological resilience is our best defence against pandemics, floods and food shortages. Health and resilience should be the gold standard of any thriving system. Yet they rarely show up on a balance sheet, a quarterly report or a GDP graph. And so, they're neglected. But these are the true indicators of vitality, and they need to become the new compass for how we design, lead and live.

But what if we returned to the root?

What if we remembered that companies are made up of biological beings that thrive in healthy ecosystems?

What if, like microbes enriching the soil, a company's role was to contribute to the health and vitality of the systems it belongs to?

What if organisations cultivated environments where people could bring their full humanity to work – their gifts, their creativity and care – in service of something much larger than themselves?

What if we designed our businesses to echo Nature's cycles and wisdom, creating the conditions for abundance, where the wellbeing of each part strengthens the whole?

What if we chose to create a new paradigm of business model, rooted in reciprocity, resilience and a reverence for life, that restores more than it takes?

What if business success was measured not just by its own bottom line but by how well it contributes to the thriving of all life, recognising that it's smart business to nurture the ecosystems that feed it?

What if limited companies embraced unlimited responsibility – to people, to planet, to future generations – becoming stewards of life rather than mere owners of assets?

What if our companies existed at this urgent moment not just to generate profit, but to serve life, to become catalysts for renewal, reconnection and right relationship with the living world?

Imagine the potential for healing, for the thriving across all life.

Companies, as dynamic organisms made up of creative people with imagination, values and agency, are the perfect vessels to make a positive impact and drive true change. And unlike a static system, a business adapts and evolves daily through its decision-making, relationships and culture. With its ability to respond in real time to the needs of its community, ecosystems and employees, it is uniquely positioned to mobilise resources, shape narratives and influence behaviour at scale. Companies have the potential to become powerful forces for regeneration, not just sustaining life but actively enriching it. Because whether we recognise it or not, business is, in its essence, a perfect microcosm of the wider ecosystem – made up of living, breathing beings who come from Nature and are inseparable from Her.

To forget this – to reduce business to numbers, endless extraction and isolated outcomes – is to imperil not just the business itself but the broader web of life it depends upon. The true purpose of business, at its most essential, is to meet real needs, support life and contribute to the collective wellbeing.

So, this is our invitation. To remember that we are not separate from Nature, but an expression of Her. That our life, our work, our business, our unique gifts, all hold the potential to nourish something beyond ourselves.

We don't need to have it all figured out. We just need to begin. To start where we are. To follow what feels alive. To tend to what feels true.

Because when we align our purpose with the needs of the world, we become part of the most important story of our time.

CHAPTER 3

All the Seasons

'If I had influence with the good fairy who is supposed to preside over the christening of all children I should ask that her gift to each child in the world be a sense of wonder so indestructible that it would last throughout life.'

Rachel Carson, *The Sense of Wonder*

For as long as I can remember, I have felt things deeply: sounds, light, the mood of the room, the feelings of people and animals, the often sad stream of news stories on the radio in my parents' kitchen. This sensitivity and empathy for injustice, and a deep attunement to what was going on around me, were not traits particularly understood in the stoic no-nonsense 1980s Ireland I grew up in, where toughening up was an armour that was seen as necessary for the world we lived in. I know now that this sensitivity to life was a kind of gift I was given, an inner radar to intuit the world around me and to respond to with creativity and with solutions.

If I close my eyes and journey back through time, it's to a scene in my childhood back garden in Dublin. I'm lying on a leopard-print picnic blanket in the shade of a cherry tree, my baby feet reaching for its branches above me as they sway in unison with the leaves dancing in the soft rhythm of summer's breeze. The dappled light casts leaf shadows on my chubby limbs. This is my earliest memory. Beyond our back wall lies the Phoenix Park, a vast sprawling expanse of Nature that stretched farther than my little mind could ever fathom. It was not just the largest enclosed park in Europe but a generational sanctuary, a place where my mother and her ten siblings had grown up exploring its every corner. And soon it would become my playground too.

As an only child for my first five years, my imagination was my closest companion, and our back garden a universe: an infinite landscape alive with possibility. Behind every tree and laurel bush new worlds awaited – places that existed just beyond the veil of reality.

When my baby sister was born, we moved to a roomier house in South County Dublin. My new bedroom, no longer a pokey box room, was now filled with light and floor space, and became a bigger canvas for my imagination as I began creating miniature indoor worlds for my toys. What started with hauling toy wooden dressers and tiny beds and placing them into new layouts for my teddies and dolls, soon evolved into reimagining my own bedroom. I would spend hours dragging furniture into different positions, draping whatever fabric I could find over my bed – even using coloured tablecloths from my mum's linen cupboard as bedcovers – to switch up the mood, painting little pictures to match the evolving themes and finishing up by picking small posies of flowers for my bedside table. I can really remember the tangible feeling of transformation and the energy shifts that came with each change. The reveal at the end of the day, when I'd made my final tweaks and called my parents in to show them, always brought their unconditional praise, however chaotic the final result turned out. And for me, even then it was really about the buzz of the process.

Over the next few years, this early fascination with interiors expanded. On playdates at my friends' elegant homes, I'd often beg them to play the game of rearranging their bedroom. It was like a childhood version of *Changing Rooms* – where the room became the canvas and beauty was the goal – but, really, I loved the creative act the most. At the beautiful Georgian homes of my aunties, I would lose myself in the soft peaches and creams of their Colefax and Fowler-inspired interiors, where I could often be found cross-legged on the floor engrossed in the stacks of 1980s *House and Garden* magazines. Their love for the aesthetic had been passed down from my grandmother, and here it was starting to flicker in me.

The act of creating was constant in my early years. I painted, knitted, and wrote poems, short stories and plays prolifically, my hands trying their best to keep up with what was flowing from my imagination. As I settled into my new neighbourhood, I found that our street teemed with girls my own age. Between games of hopscotch and Tip the Can, we cleared out my parents' garage, decorated it with homemade bunting and balloons, and filled it with my art materials and a long paint-splattered table perfect for crafting on that took up most of the space. This humble garage became a buzzing art studio for our new girl gang, the scent of interior paints and turpentine mingling with the smell of fresh paper and markers. It was a scrappy, make-do den of creativity, where we hosted our own clubs, and painted and crafted with borrowed brushes, old jars and big imaginations.

When the warmer weather arrived, we flung open the garage doors to hold Easter and summer fairs that spilled out into the front driveway. Without thinking much about it, I seemed to take a lead naturally, organising production lines, setting deadlines and making sure everything was ready for the big day. This was the late 1980s, and every penny raised went to charity, often for the children in Ethiopia, whose situation left a deep cultural mark in Ireland and felt so unfair beside our own privileged lives. I remember selling Dad's bike at one Easter fair without his knowledge, just to boost our donations. Afterwards, when the proceeds were lodged in the charity bank account, we would proudly display a giant replica cheque of the amount raised on the front gate. Looking back, those early years of collective creativity were when I felt most alive – they lit me up in a way nothing else did. Without realising it, I was learning to bring people together and to gently lead us to a common goal. I suppose it was the first flickers of purpose, lit through play and possibility.

My faculty of wonder and creativity began to dim as I entered my teenage years, with academic choices gradually taking precedence over artistic ones. My parents placed a high value on intellectual rigour; they saw education as a path to freedom, and I was proving to be a competent student. At thirteen, my school announced we'd be entering a national competition called the Young Entrepreneur of Ireland. I decided that my idea would be to reimagine the dull, plain, plastic copybook covers we all used, and redesign them with the logos of my favourite brands. I was a typical, brand-obsessed teenager and, spotting what I believed was a gap in the market, I threw myself into the project. I approached a thirteen-year-old's dream list of companies in the 1990s – Levi's, Adidas, Pepe Jeans, Nike – writing to them each by hand to pitch the idea of using their logos as advertising on the copybook covers.

My thinking was that us kids would have a stationery upgrade, and for the brands themselves it was an opportunity to be front and centre in our classrooms (as if they weren't already). One by one, the letters arrived. Branded envelopes with my name on them would be waiting for me when I came home from school. One by one, I ripped them open to find effusive, encouraging messages – and then, inevitably, a polite decline.

Crestfallen and close to giving up, I started to doubt whether the idea had even been good at all. But somewhere in that fog of disappointment, I started doodling. It was 1994, the summer of the World Cup. Like the rest of Ireland (including my classmates), I was football mad and was captain of a girls' football team. I sketched up a caricature of a footballer called Famous Seamus and, with a small loan from my parents, decided to create my own brand, screen-printing him onto copybook covers. I dropped boxes of them into local newsagents on a sale-or-return basis. To my surprise, they sold. More were wanted. Orders started coming in. To my even greater surprise, I went on to win the city, regional and, finally, the national Young Entrepreneur of Ireland. Not, I think, because the business was particularly brilliant, but because the judges saw that I allowed disappointment to redirect me, not defeat me. I hadn't given up.

And then, the bottom fell out of my world. At the end of what had been a perfect summer, aged fifteen, my parents announced we were moving to Spain. Immediately. My dad had accepted a five-year contract with the European Union Intellectual Property Office in Alicante. Within weeks, we'd packed up and gone. I was enrolled in a private Catholic school where no one spoke English. At such a tender, self-conscious age, I was an alien in every way. Overnight, I went from being popular to friendless; from being smart to being perceived as stupid. My Spanish schoolmates took down everything – my accent, my outfits, my hairstyle – until slowly, my self-worth began to unravel as my identity was picked apart. I remember sitting on the beach, watching the waves roll in, trying to resist the darkest of thoughts. I was alone. Heartbroken for the life I had lost.

I begged my parents to let me return to Dublin – to stay with an aunt, to go to boarding school, anything. Eventually, they agreed to one of my proposals (most definitely because it sounded impossible): I could leave school and spend a year teaching myself A-levels from my desk at home and, if I got the grades I needed, I could return to Dublin to start university. The challenge was steep: two years of syllabus in one, with no teachers. And I wasn't aiming low. I'd set my sights on reading Law at Trinity College, Dublin. I'd grown up watching my dad enjoy his work as a barrister. I shared his sense of justice. Without any prompting from him – in fact, he really tried hard to put me off law – I decided it was for me as well. Trinity, too, held a mythic quality: a walled fortress in the middle of the city of Dublin. My older cousins' cool, sophisticated friends studied there.

That year – and the one preceding it – really took its toll. I was depleted: socially, creatively, spiritually. My confidence and sense of self were deeply eroded, even lost, and it would take years to find my way back to the truest version of myself. But it ended on a high: in August, a letter arrived with the offer of a place to study Law at Trinity. I had done it. Against the odds. I was free to return to Dublin. Back to the people who knew and understood me, back to the seasons and the landscape I didn't realise that I loved so much until I missed them, and back to being in tune with the world around me and my own inner rhythms.

———

Of course, my dad had been right all along. Law wasn't for me. But it was something I had to find out for myself. Early in the degree, I realised that my heart just wasn't in it. The lectures felt too rigid, too black-and-white for someone who naturally dwelled in a more colourful, intuitive world. I felt like I was going against my grain.

Years later, I would come across the concept of the Rights of Nature: the idea that rivers, forests and ecosystems could be granted legal personhood and protected not as resources but as living entities with their own intrinsic rights. This use of law blew my mind. For the first time, I saw how the law could be used with imagination: as a tool for Nature protection, using the scale of justice as a lever to restore equilibrium in our ecosystems. It sparked in me a renewed interest in law, not as a career path but as a powerful language, one that could really serve life rather than control it.

Eventually, after a couple of years of forcing myself down a path that felt so far away from mine, I dropped out. I felt untethered, disappointed in myself, disoriented about my future – a high-achieving student turned college dropout, unsure of what might come next. I found myself working in a small vintage shop called The Harlequin in Dublin, where the mother-and-daughter owners took me under their wing like kind mother hens, giving me some much-needed direction.

As trust in me grew, over time they allowed me to dress the store mannequins and then the shop front window and, eventually, to help buy stock for the store. When the pieces I selected sold quickly, I started to pay more attention to what people were drawn to, what people wanted. There was something thrilling about the alchemy of it – when the right person matched to the right piece at the right moment. It was the time of Boho fashion – every girl in Dublin was wearing low-slung rah-rah skirts and suede boots. On trips to Spain to visit my parents' home, I wandered through the leather markets, drawn to the quality and craftsmanship of the same buttery suede moccasin boots that were popping up on the catwalks. I decided to bring some pairs back to the shop and put them in the window. They sold almost immediately. Encouraged, I kept sourcing more, and each time they disappeared just as fast.

Susan and Fiona, the owners, recognised in me an eye for detail and an instinct for what people wanted to buy even before I could see it myself. They saw my growing potential and, rather than hold me back, encouraged me to think bigger and to see a future beyond the walls of The Harlequin. And although they knew that nudging me would mean losing me in the shop, they cared more about helping me realise my potential than keeping me in place. And I am forever grateful for that push, and for the belief they had in me when mine was rock-bottom. The right level of encouragement, given at the right moment, can change everything. It did for me. For the first time in a long time, possibility began to bury the self-doubt. I'd found a path that felt like it could really be mine. I still carry this memory with me whenever I recognise someone's gifts and talents, remembering to nudge them towards the path they should explore if they're not already on it, even if it sometimes means letting them go.

Before long, I found myself as a trainee buyer cutting my teeth for Ireland's largest retailer, Dunnes Stores, suited and booted and travelling across the globe on buying trips, trailing behind my seniors, lugging their suitcases through airports and hotel lobbies, observing and absorbing as they engaged in the age-old ritual of haggling with suppliers. It was worlds away from the glamour of trendsetting runways and delicious materials that I had imagined.

Instead, it was a mass-market operation, the kind of retailer that was a trusted go-to for families across Ireland. But it was a good training ground for me in the business of retail, a place to learn the mechanics of buying, to understand margins, forecasting, negotiations and supply chains.

Supplier meetings were carefully choreographed: cordial, even warm on the surface, with handshakes, gifts and long dinners. But beneath the pleasantries, there was a clear power dynamic, with the retailer often in the driving seat. I quickly learned the real game: we had the power to make or break a supplier's business. Orders were often placed in the hundreds of thousands, the buyer dictating the exact price they needed – a price that would ensure they could quadruple the cost before it hit the high street. Every penny shaved off production meant millions in profit at the top.

In the beginning, I naively thought this was the science of business – a system built on logic, efficiency and numbers. But, as I sat in supplier meetings, reducing people's labour to cents, unease crept in. What did these deals mean for the workers whose factories I walked around? I watched desperate suppliers accept impossibly low margins, their livelihoods hanging in the balance. If they were under this pressure, what about the factory workers – the invisible hands working long hours, day after day, stitching together our profits? The calculations were ruthless: a few cents shaved off here, a bulk order leveraged there, just to maximise profits that would never reach the workers who made the clothes. The system demanded more, faster, cheaper. And at the top, untouched, often sat the multimillionaire retail families, reaping the rewards of an empire built on extraction.

This story wasn't at all unique – it played out across every major retail empire, woven into the DNA of capitalism's new saviour: fast fashion. This was a system built on speed, exploitation and relentless growth, where profit reigned supreme, and the true cost was buried in the factories, the supply chains and the lives of those at the bottom, and with no thought given to the impact on Nature.

That consequence didn't even register with me until a bit later, when I began to understand the full scale of the damage. Especially coming from the nurturing bosom of The Harlequin family, Dunnes was an intimidating environment to work in. Pressure and blame flowed downwards, and like the other juniors, I became a convenient scapegoat for company mistakes. My manager was simply passing down the blame, deflecting what had been forced onto her by those at the top – executives and shareholders obsessed with profit margins, setting impossible targets, the ramifications of which rippled through the company. The weight rolled downhill, each layer of management offloading it onto the next, until it reached those with the least power to push back. The store employees feared the regional managers, the regional managers feared the corporate office, and even senior buyers and directors, seemingly powerful, lived in dread of the next quarterly report that could render them obsolete. The entire system ran on anxiety, designed to extract the most while offering the least in return.

A couple of years into my job, I had saved up enough for a deposit on a fixer-upper – an ex-council house in the centre of Dublin. The house and project quickly became a creative refuge for me. After a childhood of pitching my bedroom ideas to my parents and then getting inventive with fabric draping and lava lamps in student houseshares, the thought of having my own blank canvas filled me with sheer joy. I named my house 'Woodstock', a nod to the 1960s art nouveau, psychedelic interiors mood that I unleashed on it with wild abandon; an aesthetic that mirrored my own moddish Biba-influenced look at the time. At the end of a long day at work, I would strip walls, paint and twirl through my little palace to the raw, pulsing soundtrack of PJ Harvey at full blast, fuelled by the intoxicating rush of creative freedom, coffee and cigarettes. Woodstock was my sanctuary, my outlet, my ever-beating heart.

Wallpaper had forever captivated me. As a child, I would drift off to sleep in the enchanted garden scenes that repeated across my bedroom walls, as they wove themselves into my dreams at night. That fascination never faded. When I bought Woodstock, I saved up for three rolls of William Morris wallpaper, carefully ordered from Liberty in London – a splurge that felt like an art investment at the time. I remember like it was yesterday the sheer thrill of receiving the package – the soft, creamy handle of the paper as I unrolled it so carefully, and the almost sacred precision of measuring each piece, terrified of making a wrong cut. My dad helped me hang it, and together we watched as the bland, lining-papered walls bloomed into an art nouveau dreamscape, transforming the space in soft teals and green paisleys into a cosmic garden.

Beyond dabbling in the metamorphosis of interiors, music was a passion that was lit during my Trinity days. In the early 2000s, the Irish music industry was a hotbed of talent. Dublin's scene was intimate enough to offer a front-row seat to it, and we were granted easy access to both rising Irish acts and global bands passing through. I threw myself into it completely. Music was my soul tonic – a much-needed balm to the toxic work culture I endured by day. And this tribe – a motley crew of mods, goths, ravers and singer-songwriters – became my creative family, the people who made the city come alive for me.

With the paint finally dry on my house, nights were spent at gigs, supporting friends and soaking up the scene. More and more UK A&R (artists and repertoire) executives – the talent scouts of the music industry – began flying in to discover Irish acts and, as record deals started materialising, I noticed that something was missing. Dublin lacked a multi-band music festival that truly showcased its thriving underground scene, like South by Southwest in Austin,

Texas, or In the City in Manchester. So, with my boyfriend at the time, I decided to create one. Like every venture I've ever pursued, profit was never the point – it was about creating something I wanted to exist, something I wanted to experience, but didn't yet. It was about bringing creative people together to make stuff happen and having fun in the process.

And that's exactly what the festival did. Hard Working Class Heroes became a credible showcase of the Irish music scene and a launchpad for emerging talent. It taught me so much – how to write a business plan, the importance of brand, how to organise people (this time as a young adult), manage production and the sheer energy and tenacity needed to build something from the ground up. I remember being taken to breakfast by John Reynolds, one of Ireland's most influential music promoters, curious about these young upstarts who were threatening his festival empire. From the festival, I dipped my toe in band management as another after-work creative outlet that I needed at a molecular level. Every experience expanded my horizons and community, sharpened my instincts and reinforced what I had always known – that my passion lay in creating, in bringing people together and in birthing new ideas.

———

A year into being a trainee buyer for the retailer, I had the good fortune of catching the attention of Michael, the director son of the family, when I applied for a role within the in-house boutique label he headed up. Michael was everything the wider culture was not: a culture he was probably oblivious to considering his position. He was kind and non-hierarchical and genuinely interested in the people he worked with. He seemed to really value my opinion on what young women wanted to wear, as I was the demographic, entrusting me to make the collection edits.

Working with Michael opened my eyes to a different model of supplier relationship built on mutual respect and rewards. He took me to visit small artisanal factories across Europe, where I saw an alternative to the Far Eastern mass-production model I had assumed was the industry norm. These factories produced small quantities of great quality, at fixed prices that built in a workable system with fair payment terms that benefited both parties rather than exploiting one.

In 2003, on one of our trips, we stopped off in London, where Michael, knowing my love of fashion and music, wanted to show me what he described as the holy grail of where these two worlds converged – the legendary Topshop at 214 Oxford Street. Topshop had not yet arrived in Dublin and stepping inside for the first time felt like what I imagine it was like to walk into Biba in the 1970s – a place that wasn't just a store, but a cultural epicentre – a club and a catwalk all in one. The sheer scale, the energy, the music, the subcultures, the way trends were curated and presented – it completely blew my mind. It was more than retail; it was an experience, a movement. How could I go back to bland retail after this technicolour trip?

London felt like the hottest place in the world – or, at least, it was the nexus of everything I loved. I found myself living for the next London trip, supporting my boyfriend's band at their London gigs, inhaling the raw energy of the East End and devouring every issue of *British Vogue* and *Dazed* to keep my finger on the pulse of London when I had to return to Dublin.

When my relationship ended, Dublin began to feel like a small pond. I'd put in my time at Dunnes, built my CV, and learned what I needed to learn. Dublin had revived me, shaped me, held me and got me back on track, but London was seducing me. A little black notebook I recently found in a box from that time had a note to self, scrawled on its inner cover: *'Never fight shy of the adventure. Always follow your fascination. For in your fascination, you will follow your story.'*

———

A few months later, I could be found sitting cross-legged on the floor of the Topshop buying office, just behind Oxford Street, feeling my way through the piles of soft Italian wools and French bouclés and allocating them to the jaunty tailoring sketches my designer presented me with. I had died and gone to heaven.

The office surged with the same kinetic energy that radiated from the 214 Oxford Street flagship store, and I realised that this same raw energy was being distilled into product and customer experience: fast, instinctive and plugged into the zeitgeist. For the first time, I found myself in a work environment where I didn't stick out. Everyone looked like me, only even edgier with sharper eyeliner and better haircuts.

But beyond those first superficial impressions of style, it became clear that the head office was a trove of talent and creativity. And everyone, from the most junior buying assistant to senior leadership, had a voice. It was obvious early on that input was welcomed at every level – and was actually a requirement of the job because Topshop was home to so many different style tribes, all of whom needed to be represented.

This was 2004 – a time when Topshop reigned supreme. Before it had any competition of note, before the onslaught of British high-street fashion, and when the team was a hotbed of talent at every level. I soon cast off the shackles of my experience and started to learn by osmosis how a culture could operate successfully without much hierarchy; how work could be fulfilling; how supplier relationships could be friendships. At the helm was our matriarch Jane Shepherdson, who set the tone and the agenda with her emphasis on culture, innovation, relationships – and fun!

Jane was the driving force behind Topshop's transformation from a basic high-street chain into a global fashion powerhouse. Canny and caring in equal measure, she redefined the parameters of a high-street brand and, through some visionary moves, she gave Topshop a bold new identity that made it the go-to destination for fashion-forward young women and, really, for everyone.

Jane made Topshop not just relevant, but covetable. One of her smartest moves was in 2005 when Topshop began to sponsor London Fashion Week, putting it firmly on the map. It led to Topshop's own catwalk show, which started to set its own trends. Suddenly, the brand was mentioned in the same breath as Miu Miu and Marc Jacobs and the exciting new wave of young British designers. Topshop trends appeared on the pages of *Vogue*. It was cool to say you shopped at Topshop regardless of whether you could afford a designer price tag; the fact that whatever your socioeconomic background you could save up a little and buy a piece that was worn by fashion editors, musicians, models and actors made everyone wear their Topshop wardrobe with pride.

She was also deeply committed to nurturing the emerging talent of new generation designers and, as these young designers became friends of the brand, I remember them being mentored, financially supported, even helped with their production needs. These friendships became partnerships that led to some of the first-ever high-street/designer collaborations: Christopher Kane, Jonathan Saunders, Marios Schwab, Richard Nicoll. It was visionary. It gave designers the financial leg-up they needed, and it was, of course, a cool brand coup for Topshop. These partnerships changed the industry.

Jane's vision was never about optics or any kind of surface-level branding or greenwashing. It came from a place of genuine care and concern – she cared about the product, the hands that made it, and the journey it took to reach the catwalk or the shop floor. Long before sustainability became an industry concern, Jane was starting to bring ethics into Topshop's DNA as she spearheaded initiatives like Topshop's first Fair Trade collection, championing sustainable fabrics, and pushing for ethically produced denim and recycled materials before it was fashionable.

She demanded much more transparency from the supply chain and started to pioneer what was then quite a radical idea – that high-street fashion could be both trend-led and ethically conscious. Her early commitment to sustainability really set a precedent as she showed that doing good didn't mean compromising on style – or success. Jane understood innately that a brand's MO wasn't just to sell clothes but to inspire and empower. She was the first person to really plant the seed in me that business could be a force for good. And her legacy continues to influence how brands balance style with responsibility in today's evolving retail landscape. I soaked up all of it and learned on the job. Topshop became my university – and although it was in the early days of sustainability, I saw a universe where commerce and creativity and purpose could coexist side by side.

Those were heady days of working hard and playing harder, and I found a real sisterhood in the girls I worked with there, who became lifelong friends. I gravitated towards the design team, where there was little ego or hierarchy, and we shared an intuition for colour, shapes and beautiful materials. It was the type of collaborative environment that I thrived in, and I was back once again to my parents' garage, dreaming up new creations with my friends.

Our task was to use our inner intuition like a crystal ball – to spot the trends on the street before they made it to the catwalk. We took the brief seriously, armed with our digital cameras on nights out pubbing and clubbing, always on alert for an original detail, a new silhouette, a fresh colour story. We were dispatched to all the major UK and global music festivals, put on the beat to mine the fields for inspiration. Trends weren't born in boardrooms; they were born on the streets and in the clubs, and we were the youth, we were the customer. Keeping our finger on the pulse wasn't just encouraged – it was a requirement of the role to bottle those moods, translate them into collections and keep the brand at the forefront of direction. It was amazing to feel that my whole identity – me being me – was also my job.

I was lucky to have caught this special moment at Topshop before the winds changed. But change inevitably crept in. Subtly at first, then impossible to ignore. Philip Green, the retail tycoon who had bought Topshop in 2002, started to take a closer interest in the business. In the beginning, he was too busy with the rest of the Arcadia brands he'd acquired in the deal, and he left Jane and our team to it. We had free rein. The formula was working. We were smashing targets. Topshop was the hottest brand in the world. Why fix what wasn't broken? Yet the demand for ever-greater profits and faster growth soon began to shape decisions at the top, even if it meant tampering with what had made the brand successful in the first place. From our perspective, it felt short-sighted – a kind of false economy. What wasn't recognised was that, like any ecosystem, everything is connected and if you change one thing, you shake the whole foundation. And when that balance is upset, the fallout is inevitable.

Philip wasn't the type to be kept at arm's length, and the new leadership began to insert itself directly into our seasonal buying presentations. It no longer seemed to be about the creative vision or the trends, or the beautiful fabrics we had so carefully sourced. The conversation now narrowed to the numbers as the margins were demanded and we were told that we were paying too much. With little room to refuse, production gradually shifted to countries such as China, Bangladesh and Turkey. Materials became cheaper and more generic, and the quality and standards that had once underpinned Topshop's credibility began to erode.

Philip's background was in trading – fast deals, quick profits and an instinct for what would sell. That approach had built his empire. But, in my experience, running a global fashion brand requires more than trading instinct; it relies on brand integrity, customer loyalty and a sense of community. It's about knowing when to invest rather than just cut costs. And when cost-cutting trumped investment in creativity and quality, the DNA of Topshop changed.

It wasn't long before the consequences of these moves began to surface. Media reports started to raise concerns about low wages and poor conditions in some of the factories supplying Topshop, and the brand's once-impeccable reputation took a hit. A company that had been pioneering ethics in fashion suddenly found itself on the wrong side of the conversation. For us, watching sustainability fall off the agenda in favour of ever-faster production cycles and disposable fashion trends felt like a catastrophic misstep.

Jane had so carefully built Topshop's success by curating trend-driven fashion while cultivating a cool, aspirational image. But now, her vision increasingly clashed with the hands-on, cost-focused approach from the top. As Philip focused on rapid expansion, celebrity-courting and profit margins, Jane tried to maintain the brand's credibility as a trend-setter rather than just another mass-market retailer. She believed in quality, design and originality, whereas Philip's primary focus seemed to be on ever-growing profitability.

Still, it was a shock when Jane announced her resignation. She had fought the fights for the brand, and for us, but she couldn't walk any further on a path she didn't believe in. We wept. To us, the soul of the Topshop we lived and breathed for had been ripped away.

And looking back now, it was the beginning of the end. The brand that had once defined fashion was now on a downward spiral. The team did their best to keep the vision and DNA of the Topshop we knew and loved alive, but the grip from the top was too tight.

In our eyes, it was only a matter of time before we watched it slowly suffocate.*

---

* In spring 2025, at a reunion organised by Jane in the Fitzrovia pub where we used to start our Friday nights, and the first time we'd all been together since those heady days, the topic of the night was the day's headlines: Topshop was returning. At that point, it was just a tease on social media, cryptic posts bearing messages like 'We missed you too' and 'We've been listening', hinting at something big brewing behind the scenes. None of us old-timers had any idea who was behind it, and from the imagery it didn't seem to bear any of the hallmarks of the Topshop we once knew and loved. Since then, Topshop's relaunch has become real. By early 2026, the brand is set to return to physical retail, selling in thirty-two John Lewis stores across the UK and marking a clear step back into high-street territory. But despite the theatrical comeback, its critics are watching. *Vogue Business* points out that Topshop's return feels suffused with 'business as usual' and with very little transparency about sourcing, wages or sustainable design, and no clear movement beyond what feels like nostalgia packaged for consumption. It's not a return of its legacy or of the soul of the brand that mattered so much to many – the ethical core, the creative integrity is still absent. I don't think there would have been a House of Hackney without having experienced Topshop. But while that story belongs to the past as a crucible, ours is a reminder that new models can carry the baton forwards.

First Nature

'In our every deliberation, we must consider the impact on the seventh generation.'

Principle based on the Haudenosaunee
Confederacy's 'Great Law of Peace'

My experience of Topshop was day and night: I saw it at its most visionary, and at its most destructive. Both sides of the coin taught me so much about business: how to be, and how not to be. Experiencing both extremes was instrumental in conjuring up the kind of brand Javvy and I would eventually create – crystallising what to bring forwards and what to consciously leave behind.

I carried with me the best of what I'd seen: a culture rooted in soft, feminine power – nurturing, collaborative, intuitive. A leader who inspired ethics, innovation, creativity and relationships – showing us that success didn't have to come at the expense of others. And then I witnessed its opposite: a culture led by a dictating force, driven by ego and greed, culminating in the loss of thousands of jobs, people discarded like last season's stock. There were deep lessons in all of it.

But, beneath all of this, and far beyond my twenty-something, self-centred awareness, lay another truth. The high-street model, in its very design, was extractive. Built on overproduction, underpayment and speed, it demanded a relentless churn of product that came at the hidden cost of vast environmental degradation. Entire ecosystems were disrupted to produce cheap cotton, rivers were polluted by toxic dyes, synthetic fibres leached microplastics into the ocean and mountains of unsold clothes became destined for landfill or incineration. It was a system that had no consideration for the costs or consequences for Nature, including the welfare of humans within it, and none of us were talking about it. We were too caught up in the thrill – the trends, the turnover, the illusion of endless growth. The high-street fast-fashion model was celebrated as an economic success story, a triumph of efficiency and affordability. No one was publicly questioning it because this was the only model we knew: the glossy storefronts, the seasonal collections, the racks of ever-changing trends – all of it relied on a system that prioritised the highest profit and the fastest growth as the pinnacle of success.

And yet, I was complicit. We all were. It would take me a couple more years before I started the journey of considering the world beyond myself, and beyond my own lifetime. That awakening came with the birth of our son. As he slept in my arms, I portalled into his future and the future of his generation. In those lucid moments the deep remembrance came to me that it is our responsibility to leave the world in good shape for our children, current and future. That we are only ever caretakers – a role passed down through generations – and it is our sacred ancestral job to caretake well.

Once I saw it, I couldn't unsee it. Once I knew, I couldn't unknow. I had to leave fast fashion fast, and the mindset that fed it, and start searching for another way.

———

There were dancefloor whispers in The Dolphin pub that night about a warehouse rave in Enterprise House, one of the original live/work spaces where creatives shot fashion editorials by day and threw brilliant parties by night. When the bright lights came on and the night was yet young to us seasoned Topshop girls, we slinked over to Enterprise House. I remember climbing the fire door stairs and feeling it in my chest first: the pulsing bassline synths and Annie Lennox vocals reverberating through the cavernous space. As we walked in, a choreographed vision unfolded before us – beautiful people moving in rhythmic groove, dappled in pink strobe lights. The atmosphere was electrifying. Yes, sweet dreams *are* made of this.

Time blurred. Boundaries dissolved. Tune after tune, the DJ took us on a journey of unexpected 80s synth B-sides, obscure gems that were personal favourites, like a curated soundscape made especially for me. He controlled the pulse of the room, shaping our contours like a master wizard weaving spells through sound. It was one of the best sets I'd ever experienced. *Dreams Never End.** Somewhere in the blur of sound and light, I found myself striking up a conversation with the DJ over the music. Javvy was his name. It sounded like Javi – a name I'd always liked when I lived in Spain. We connected firstly on a music level. And then came the next level. I can only describe meeting Javvy as being like a homecoming. It was like a visceral memory, a soul recognition; like we'd loved each other in another life and had finally found our way back. Three months later, he moved into my house.

Within a year of meeting, Javvy proposed. Soon after, I was promoted to buyer for the Kate Moss range. It was a few seasons into her Topshop collaboration and Kate was adored by everyone lucky enough to work with her. I was a huge fan – of her, and of the legendary stylist Katy England, who co-created the collection. I couldn't have been more excited. It was in Bali on a sourcing trip for the collection when I first began to feel unwell. I assumed it was a bug I'd picked up and starved myself for three weeks, hoping it would pass. But the nausea only got worse and worse. When I got home and visited my GP, skinny and depleted, he suggested a pregnancy test. Lo and behold, I was twelve weeks pregnant.

It was unexpected but very happy news – except that I had become a husk of myself. I prayed the symptoms would ease, once the hormones supposedly settled, but they only intensified. There was no relief – sixteen weeks came and went, then twenty, and still I was relentlessly sick. I dragged myself to work every day, the smells of Soho hitting me like a wall and making me throw up the moment I got off the bus (the Tube was completely off limits to me).

---

* New Order, 'Dreams Never End', on *Movement*, Factory Records, 1981, vinyl.

Morning sickness is a cruel misnomer – mine clung to me day and night. I had just been promoted into a high-visibility role and felt under immense pressure to perform, though I had resigned myself to the fact that Kate and I would sadly not be sipping cocktails at The Dorchester. One day, we took a helicopter together to visit a vintage archive in Dorset. I sat beside her up in the sky, eyes closed, stomach churning to the whirring of the chopper, silently willing every molecule of my body to please not be sick on Kate Moss. She was so sweet and sympathetic – feeding me pizza when we got to the archive to ease the nausea – but others weren't so understanding. A director, who was equally pregnant but glowing, found me one afternoon with my head down on my desk, green at the gills, while everyone else was upstairs at a company presentation in the canteen. I explained how ill I felt, but in turn she chided me for not going up for it. Woman to woman. Not pregnant woman to pregnant woman. The lack of empathy or understanding was really upsetting. I was too low in energy and confidence, too focused on just getting through the day to speak up. But looking back, it was a deeply disappointing way to handle something so natural, especially in a female-led workplace.

Philip stayed very close to the Kate Moss collection, and my symptoms were viewed less as something to support and more as a liability to performance and sales. Eventually, I was quietly reassigned to an 'easier' department: Topshop Maternity. Going from the cachet of the Kate Moss collection to designing frumpy maternity wear felt like a complete demotion. My confidence plummeted, and with a heightened sensitivity and the growing weight of a responsibility that extended now beyond myself, I began to really worry about my place and my future at Topshop.

But, as is so often the case, what felt like a career setback at the time would eventually reveal itself to be a blessing in disguise. The departmental change brought a spell of creative stagnation that contrasted with the intense stimulation and sheer workload of the previous four years. Yet, amidst the lull, I found an unexpected joy in designing clothes that made pregnant women feel beautiful, knowing firsthand that pregnancy isn't always a glowing experience. With it being a small capsule collection, I had more time than I had used to and soon I could do the job in my sleep. It gave me space to think, to rest, to dream again.

The boredom and space became a fertile ground for my imagination to wake up and stretch beyond the limits of my current reality. It remains one of my life regrets that I raced back to work when my baby son, Javi, was just shy of three months old. After a horrendous pregnancy and what felt like a lack of support – whether real or imagined – I returned early, feeling fragile and unsure of my footing. I didn't feel my career could afford the risk of being out of the business any longer. Maternity provision was minimal, and the culture did little to encourage time out. Topshop offered financial incentives to return early, a policy that, while technically optional, sent a clear message to new mothers: a quick return was not just welcomed, it was expected.

That experience, paired with my growing understanding of just how critical the mother–child bond is during the first few months, became the catalyst for one of the policies I'm most proud of at House of Hackney. I never wanted anyone in our team to feel the way I did: unsure of their place, pressured to return too soon, forced to choose between financial stability and their child's needs at the most sensitive time. So we created a maternity leave policy that honours the precious fourth trimester and beyond – a time when, as Nature intended, mothers and babies are meant to remain closely attached in a bond that's not just emotionally vital but biologically essential (a mother's physical presence helps regulate a baby's heart rate, body temperature, stress response and even the development of their brain). Breastfeeding, skin-to-skin contact and consistent maternal proximity have profound long-term benefits for both emotional security and cognitive development. And no child should be deprived of this because of an employment contract.

Our policy mirrors that innate wisdom: nine months of maternity leave to reflect the very cycle of gestation itself – a full season of nurturing on either side of birth. With six months at full pay and three months at half pay, it is designed to honour the time, rest and security needed for the deep bonding, maternal recovery and the slow, sacred settling into life together. Because when we protect this early window, we protect something far greater – the roots from which future humans grow. Because when mothers thrive, families flourish – and so does the world.

During that short summer of maternity leave, I had a big shift in consciousness. Giving birth to a child pulls you sharply out of your own self-awareness, lifting you from your own orbit into a shared, collective one, where the centre of gravity is no longer your own life, but that of your child, and your thoughts drift to the world they will inhabit.

The future becomes more than an abstract concept as you begin to see life not just through your own eyes, but through the eyes of the generations to come. Purpose and responsibility surface in ways you could never have imagined. When our son was born, it sparked a deep awakening in Javvy and me. His birth was accompanied by a jolt of awareness of the world he would inherit, and the impact of the choices we made. It became clear that we had to align our values with our actions. That we needed to find a path that honoured our purpose and the world our child would grow up in.

Javvy had grown up in Somerset, in the West Country, and spent his 1980s childhood roaming free-range with his friends, always on a mission for adventure. Summer days were spent freewheeling their BMXs through ancient woodlands, disappearing into the trees to build bivouacs and tree houses, lighting campfires and losing themselves in the wild, before pedalling fast to make it home before their twilight curfew. I suppose you could say that Javvy was creating Nature spaces from an early age, moving through them with the kind of instinct that comes from years of exploring his playground. This is where he was completely at home.

Although I had a deep connection with Nature as a child, it felt like a distant memory – the expectations of school, then work and living in cities had pulled me indoors and quietly severed it, drawing me instead to the creative energy of the city that kept my twenties in motion. So, when for our first date Javvy took me wild camping on the Isle of Wight – me in my black leather biker jacket, my second skin back then – it was the coolest, most original date I'd ever been on. As we hiked to our pitch, he pointed out the names of the trees as he mimicked the different birdsong with a fluency that was all part of his language. That night, around our makeshift campfire, he traced the constellations with his finger, telling me their names and meanings like an ancient storyteller. I listened, completely mesmerised – not just by the vastness of the cosmos, which in my city-bound, fast-paced life I'd long forgotten to notice – but by this cosmic Nature boy for whom the stars and the trees were old friends.

It was around the campfire that night that Javvy told me he had always taken solace in Nature, a place that counterbalanced the trauma of his school years. The classroom was a daily source of shame and struggle for him. Severely dyslexic but undiagnosed, he was misunderstood as slow and was separated from the rest of the class, placed in a glass box of a room where everyone could see, in a daily humiliation. He struggled with reading and writing words, but he could design and make anything with his hands, and he knew he had a natural ability for problem-solving.

But what was supposed to be a place of growth became a place of exclusion. His mum had him at nineteen, and though his childhood was loving, it was hand to mouth, and school wasn't high on the agenda. Everything he had, he had to earn for himself. At ten years old, he got a paper round before school, rising at 6am to deliver newspapers so he could buy himself a BMX. That bike became his freedom, his escape route into Nature and the beginning of a lifelong love affair with the woods.

Javvy set his sights on university – the first in his family to even consider it – and fought hard to get there. Against all odds, he got into fashion at the University of Westminster. What followed was a total metamorphosis. A college professor there was the first to recognise his dyslexia, in a moment that changed everything. For the first time, he could start to make sense of himself. What had been perceived as a flaw was, in fact, a different kind of brilliance. The dyslexic mind, with its gift for pattern recognition, 3D-thinking and inventive problem-solving, was perfectly suited to design. So, he wasn't lacking. His intelligence was just wired differently. And that knowledge finally empowered him to embrace this difference and to bring those gifts, fully and unapologetically, into his design degree. It was the beginning of a chapter where Javvy could be finally in alignment with his true self, where he was no longer going against the grain.

Around that same time, he applied for a student bank account, and NatWest sent him a card with a printing error. It arrived with the name Javvy M. Royle instead of Jason M. Foyle. A perfect accident at the perfect moment. The name became him. Or perhaps he became the name. It marked the death of the old story, the end of the lost boy – and the birth of a new one: the beginning of the found man. A story that honoured his true nature. The joke wasn't lost on me that the universe had bestowed the name Royle upon this prince of a man – not by birth, but by becoming.

So, when the time came, we named our son Javi to honour the continuum of this new lineage.

CHAPTER 5

There's No Place like Hackney

'Beauty will save the world.'

Fyodor Dostoevsky, *The Idiot*

There was never a grand plan for House of Hackney. But all the signs pointed to a season of change for us. My first baby-faced summer of maternity leave, and its accompanying light, slowly retreated into autumn and was followed by a reluctant return to the churn of work. Winter inevitably followed: a time of introspection and reckoning, of listening to the big questions in our hearts that only surface in the stillness of a season of life like this.

We had both fallen out of love with the fashion machine – the exploitation, the disposability, the relentless pace of the model. Javvy played a big role in my awakening. After university, he cut his teeth with master designers like Alexander McQueen and Hussein Chalayan. From those experiences, he took with him a meticulous eye for detail, a reverence for craftsmanship and for a slow, more considered process. For him the way that something was made mattered just as much as how it looked. Each stitch, texture and technique carried meaning. It was the antithesis of the profit-driven speed of the industry I was in. His values ran deep, rooted in a respect for the craft, the materials and the skilled hands behind it. Through our late-night conversations between baby feeds, I began to question everything – my work, my impact, the ethics of an industry built on speed and excess. Having a child deepened that questioning even more. Legacy began to matter. We found ourselves wondering: what kind of world were we helping to create? What kind of future would our son inherit?

In stark contrast to fashion's fleeting nature, interiors were built to endure. They offered lasting worlds that stayed with me, and with those who lived among them. Worlds I had created since childhood. In my bedroom, in my mind, with fabric and dreams.

I'd settled east the moment I arrived in London from Dublin, moving into a flat just off Brick Lane to be right in the thick of the action I was so hungry for. The spirit of the East End in the early 2000s was completely intoxicating to me. It held a wild, unfiltered energy in the air – a sense that anything could happen and probably would. Before gentrification swept through it and smoothed its edges, East London belonged to the outsiders – the misfits, the makers, the outliers. I caught a fleeting moment in time, but it burned brightly.

I knew very quickly that London was my new home and that I wasn't going back to Dublin – so I sold my house there and threw myself fully into this new chapter. While Topshop was going through its own metamorphosis, I found myself more and more drawn to the world of interiors. Transforming old buildings and creating beautiful spaces made my heart beat in a way fashion never could. It was rooted deeply in my psyche – I was back again in my childhood bedroom, immersed in the creation of a new world within its four corners.

After a year of renting and getting to know East London like the back of my hand, I found a little place that had been sitting empty for months on Columbia Road. It was the depths of a bitterly cold February, and the street was stark and silent, shutters pulled down tightly on windows and the flower stalls packed away. But to me, even in midwinter, it looked like a film set waiting to be brought to life. I was utterly charmed by this little terraced house with its weathered brickwork and sash windows where, come Sunday, a street Eden would bloom just outside, the scent of eucalyptus and roses drifting through the windows like a waking dream.

Us Topshop girls were growing up. It was a time of cheap mort-gages and low deposits, and although our wages were modest, so were the barriers to buying. Somehow, between the late nights and long workdays, we began translating our creative flair and business nous into interiors. Buying, doing up and selling flats became our new hustle, and soon we all had projects on the go. As young single women navigating the building world, we shared a rolodex of trusted builders and trades. More often than not, we were on-site ourselves – hanging off ladders, paintbrushes in hand, boots caked in dust. Our homes were creative blank canvases: spaces to imagine, transform and bring to life like a collection, only more rewarding.

After Columbia Road came London Fields. I think I was drawn to it by the name alone – London Fields – there was something oxymoronic about it, the idea of fields in the heart of the city. The Fields of London. It sounded like a storybook. And somehow, it lived up to its name. It was an oasis in the middle of beautiful gritty Hackney. The juxtaposition was part of the magic – wildflower meadows and football matches, dog walkers and artists, everyone sharing this sliver of green like a big communal living room. I met Javvy just days after getting the keys to a doer-upper townhouse here – the house that would become House of Hackney.

I'd fallen for it at first sight, able to see beyond the bedsits and PVC windows to what it could become, but it was a serious project. Javvy quickly became my solid wingman in the renovation. When we met, he was working as a designer in an agency, and his fashion degree and background in pattern cutting somehow translated effortlessly into the world of interiors as he approached the task at hand with the precision of a tailor, measuring, drafting, solving spatial problems like he was laying out a garment, though he had never renovated a house before.

His skillset seemed to be everything that I lacked: he was more technical, more solution-oriented, more exacting than I was. Maybe it was my love-struck eyes, but he seemed to embody the best of an architect, electrician, plumber, carpenter and decorator, all rolled into one. Javvy poured hours of labour into the house – after work, on weekends – purely in the spirit of helping me build something I don't think I could ever have managed alone. We quickly became a team, falling in love over greasy fry-ups in local caffs before heading in for another dusty day on the tools. And little did we know then just how much that house and the life we were beginning to build inside it would go on to inspire.

That Victorian house in London Fields – the one Javvy helped me renovate – quickly became *our* home. We loved Hackney. Javvy had been part of the first wave of creative settlers in the late 1990s, attracted by cheap rents, Zone 2 access and beautiful parks. A decade later, it was starting to gentrify, but Hackney still felt like a place where anything was possible. It was the birthplace of ideas, a melting pot of cultures, a hotbed of talent and a thriving creative community with more designers per capita than anywhere else in the world. Hackney felt truly liberated and charged with energy. Diversity was celebrated. Possibility stretched as far as your imagination would take it. Hackney was open to big dreams. This kinetic spirit of Hackney and its community fuelled us endlessly and would ultimately infuse the brand.

I loved the bones of the house from the moment I first viewed it and saw the pink magnolia tree that flanked it, whose creamy petals filled the bedroom window like Nature's own curtains. It was a three-storey townhouse, simple and unassuming, built in the 1880s for London's growing working-class and lower-middle-class populations. It had no illusions of grandeur – it wasn't pretending to be more than just a solid home that had nurtured generations.

We named the house 'Loddiges' after Loddiges Nursery, one of the largest and most celebrated horticultural Victorian hothouses in Europe, which introduced countless exotic species to Britain, including palms, orchids and tropical ferns, and played a major role in influencing the development of Kew Gardens. The nursery had stood just a stone's throw from our home, though by the time we arrived it was long gone.

When the renovations were finished, we painted the interior a chalky white, as I had done time and time again with every house I'd decorated, as a backdrop to the minimalist, mid-century interior that continued to define the decade aesthetically. It was the ubiquitous blank canvas of everyone's rooms. But what once felt chic and industrial now felt clinical and cold – like living in a dental surgery, with nothing to soften the edges of the austere and tense outside world. As the mood of the late 2000s unfolded, shaped by the austerity of the post-financial crash, the world felt like a much heavier place.

Our instinct was to cocoon ourselves in Nature and pay homage to the original Loddiges. But though tall and thin, the house had only a postage-stamp-sized concrete backyard, too small to swing a cat in, let alone cultivate a mini Eden. So, we turned our attention inwards. What if instead of a garden, we wondered, we brought Nature inside the house? What if we created an interior garden, blurring the boundaries between indoors and out? We began to dream of 'living rooms' in the truest sense – spaces that felt alive and spirited. Like a painted garden brought to life, we imagined swathing the walls in botanical prints and filling it with Boston ferns and Kentia palms, letting Nature's motifs reclaim the hard edges of modernism, echoing the romance of the Victorian glasshouses that inspired the house.

But when we began the search for the Nature-infused wallpaper and textiles to drench our house in, we hit a dead end. At one end of the market was the craftsmanship and quality we aspired to use, the same fine-spun linens and buttery velvets I remembered from childhood homes – chintzy Colefax and Fowler florals, intricate William Morris patterns, rich with heritage and artistry. We knew that the quality we were looking for was to be found in Chelsea Harbour, the one-stop destination for luxury textiles. But when we got there, we discovered the Harbour was a sea of beige, reflecting the minimalist decorative mood we were, by then, bored to death of. Worse still, shopping for high-end textiles back then just wasn't accessible. You needed an interior designer with a trade account – even though we had a clear vision for our project in our heads and felt capable of bringing it to life ourselves, there was no direct-to-consumer option.

At the lower end of the market was the new phenomenon of the fast homewares model, which mirrored its predecessor, fast fashion, offering affordable, trend-driven décor at the cost of quality, sustainability and individuality. It transformed the way people furnished their homes as sleek minimalist, Scandi-inspired furniture was suddenly both affordable and accessible. Design felt democratic; everyone could now afford to change their rooms, which, in some ways, was a good thing. But what were the unseen costs? New mass-market retailers like IKEA, Made.com and H&M Home were fuelling this culture of disposable interiors, where cheaply made furniture and home accessories were designed for a short-term appeal rather than any kind of longevity. And while the affordability was enticing, the model carried catastrophic consequences. The reality was mass landfill waste. And the waste itself wasn't the only issue. Due to the diversity of materials and toxic compounds used, fast homeware is notoriously difficult to recycle; most of it simply ends up in landfill, with an estimated 22 million pieces discarded each year in the UK alone. The demand for this fast, low-cost production model pushed traditional craftsmanship and ethical labour practices to the margins, disconnecting people from the art and soul of beautifully made interiors as craftsmanship, beauty and longevity were sacrificed. Homes began to lose their uniqueness as they morphed into identikit homogenised spaces, made even more soulless by the ubiquitous white wall that backdropped nearly every interior at the time. It was a blank and expressionless canvas, that only mirrored the bleak, austere zeitgeist of this post-crash era.

But while the fashion editors continued to laud the high street on their shopping pages, a different mood started to creep into the glossy pages of *British Vogue*. Led by the work of a photographer named Tim Walker, Javvy and I noticed that a new world was beginning to unfold, where a fairytale fantasy met a topsy-turvy British aesthetic. And it felt so fresh. Tim, along with his supremely talented band of creatives, people like set designers Shona Heath and Simon Costin, created a kaleidoscopic editorial that was high on colour, wallpaper and textiles and was often set in great British houses that were stacked high with antiques, art and heirloom furniture. While everyone else was focused on the fashion in the photographs, we were enchanted by the interiors.

These were the kinds of cinematic rooms we longed to escape to, rooms swathed in a prismatic tapestry of living. A sea change from the stuffy interiors rulebook in authenticity and spirit. A subverted celebration of the past, infused with a jolly dose of fun and escapism. The past had never felt so modern. In a time marked by austerity, here was imagination, beauty and a defiance. The images cracked open a window into another world of joy, eccentricity and the beauty of imperfection.

How we wanted to live in this universe. To create a home of our own that pushed back against the disposable and the soulless – the very opposite of the high street's homogenised offering that was to this point defining the times we were living through. We began rising with the sun, to catch the train to Sunbury Antiques Market at Kempton Park. There, over scalding tea and toasties, we rediscovered the textures of time – wood carved by hands, textiles worn by life, objects that whispered of beauty and utility – an ethos William Morris captured so perfectly. They felt like keys to a forgotten language.

The silhouettes we discovered at Kempton stirred distant memories of my grandmother Peg's home. She herself was the embodiment of bold, nonconformist taste. From the outside, her semi-detached house near the gates of Phoenix Park in Dublin seemed unassuming. Inside, however, was a treasure trove – a place of enchantment for my younger self. Peg was on first-name terms with every antique dealer in Dublin, zipping between them on her motorbike in her signature Cossack hat. Yet, nothing was merely for show; every fine bone china teacup and saucer was folded into the rhythm of her household's daily rituals.

Looking back, it was there that I first resonated emotionally with an interior space. It was that exact emotional resonance we were so desperately seeking to bring into our home. Yet we couldn't find it in the shops or in the showrooms. Nature was also so noticeably absent in the mass-produced mediocrity. This vision was crystal clear to us and the clarion call for change, for disruption, for beauty, for craftsmanship, for storytelling rang louder and louder until we couldn't hear anything else but the invitation to be brave and to build it.

And so, we handed in our notices.

CHAPTER 6

Build It and They Will Come

*'Everything that is made beautiful and fair
and lovely is made for the eye of one who sees.'*

Rumi

The world didn't need yet another brand. But as we sat around our kitchen table in our house in Hackney, staring at the blank canvas we had before us, we felt the opportunity, and the responsibility, to create something radically different. We wanted to create a brand that truly moved people – aesthetically, emotionally, ethically and with a healthy dose of irreverent spirit to counteract the sombreness of the times. It had to answer the quest we'd been on all along: how to bring Nature's beauty into our homes visually but also viscerally. Through print and palette, but also through feeling. The product needed to be, in the words of William Morris, both beautiful *and* useful. Crafted by happy hands, using materials that would stand the test of time. Pieces to be lived with, loved and passed down once again. Future heirlooms, we called them.

Our plans were intentionally cottage sized. We had no desire for aggressive growth, no ambitions to build and sell, no exit strategy. House of Hackney was always meant to be small and beautiful, and we knew a fast-growth model would be at odds with this. And after the burnout and disillusionment of the corporate world, we longed for something more meaningful. We had made our way back home again.

This would be a kitchen-table business, fuelled by creative freedom and the joy of making something we truly believed in. And that, we felt, would sate us far more than any financial return ever could.

Although I longed to emulate the familiar spirit of my Nana's home, we weren't trying to recreate the past, but rather to borrow the best of it. The considered craftsmanship, the timeless silhouettes., the vibrational hum of objects that were born from a more soulful, intentional way of making. We sought to honour that integrity, but also to subvert it – to inject some humour and spirit and juxtapose the heritage of the past with the pulse of the now to create an aesthetic and a vibe that felt utterly new.

We were total newcomers to the interiors industry and didn't know the playbook – or that a playbook even existed. Instead of following stuffy rules, we set out to inspire people to decorate their own way – to create interiors that spoke to them regardless of design trends and rules. We placed ourselves in the shoes of the customer – because we were the customer. So, we created one of the first direct-to-consumer interiors websites to demystify the process of interiors shopping and instead empower people with the tools to make their own choices. We wanted everyone to enjoy the process – to be playful, experimental, and to design without having to go through a gatekeeper. To be able create sanctuaries that were as unique as the people living in them.

Alongside being outliers in the interiors world, we were launching a business without ever having studied business. The closest I'd come was the business plan I wrote in my early teens for the Young Entrepreneur of Ireland competition. But once again, without knowing the rules, without being schooled in the systems of economics, without convention or expectation, we were free from any inherited thinking.

We were free to conjure a pure, untethered vision of what we wanted House of Hackney to stand for. It was by acting on those freedoms – by not looking at the rulebook, not following trends, not trying to please anyone else, but tuning into our intuition – that we found our path.

Our guiding philosophy was to bring more joy and spirit into people's homes. Through Nature, through beauty, through imagination. And how could we bring it to life without leaving much harm in our wake, and instead leaving something better behind?

We quickly earned the title of disruptors. Some were kind enough to add the prefix 'positive'. But we weren't disrupting for disruption's sake. We weren't chasing headlines or rebelling just to be different. And we certainly weren't trying to be the enfants terribles the Chelsea set made us out to be, though we took the badge of provocateurs as a quiet compliment.

We sold Javvy's flat to fund the business and invited a handful of friends and family – those who believed in us as people and the vision we had, even without any proof of concept – to come on board with small, tax-efficient investments through the EIS (enterprise investment scheme). Between leaving our jobs and launching the brand, we gave ourselves just nine months to design a collection, find the factories to produce it, build a website and midwife House of Hackney into the world. We simply couldn't afford to be without an income for any longer than that.

Looking back now, I realise that the nine-months term we had was the same gestational period it takes to grow a human life. It wasn't long, but we were fuelled by the kind of unbridled creativity that let us finally design what our hearts wanted, without restraints or having to sell fifty thousand pieces of a product. The turbocharge of purpose fused with the adrenaline of a ticking clock powered us through the long days and nights. With no income, we lived on a shoestring, setting ourselves a strict daily budget just to eat. Every trip to the supermarket became an exercise in discipline: no luxuries, no fancy fruit. Just the absolute essentials.

Our bare-bones budget forced us to be resourceful. Javvy and I pooled our skills – every seemingly random ability we'd picked up over the years suddenly felt destined for this moment. Between us, we covered it all: designing the product, building the website, creating the brand logo and packaging. I drew on my buying background to create the mood boards, plastered with torn-out fashion editorials and the faded bohemian grandeur of houses like beautiful Port Eliot in Cornwall, and to oversee the range planning and stock assortment.

We settled on three debut collections: Dalston Rose, Hackney Empire and Queen Bee. Each had their own mood and narrative and would consist of wallpaper, fabric, cushions, furniture, lighting and bedding. The opening aesthetic was unapologetically British: romantic, Nature-steeped and edged with grunge. 'Colefax and Fowler on acid', someone called us. It was heritage, but with humour. Tradition, but subverted. A modern remix of British romanticism, shot through with irreverent spirit.

We started with the smallest production runs our factories would make. Timing was on our side. We were launching a print brand in the era of digital printing, which meant the kaleidoscopic colours of our dreams were finally possible, no longer confined by the technical limitations of traditional screen printing. With no boundaries, we could use all the hues we ever imagined, with as much intricate detail and layered depth we wanted, and, crucially, we could print in small batches. There were no vast minimums or one-colour-only restrictions or wastage. It was a revolution that had already transformed fashion, and we were poised to bring that same boundless freedom of colour into the home.

There were some steep learning curves in those early days, and one wrong move could have sounded the death knell for the company – we didn't have any buffer to make a mistake. The bedding range alone came close to nearly killing the business. It swallowed a large portion of our launch budget as it was the only product that used traditional rotary printers that required huge minimums. We later learned from the homeware buyers of luxury department stores that during recessions, people stop buying bed linen. As beautiful as it was, as utterly sublime the quality was to sleep in, it took us years to clear the stock.

We soon realised that interiors buying was very different to fashion – people needed to see, touch and feel the product. It was a far more considered purchase than a dress from Topshop, which could be tried on. We learned that people have an imagination gap when it comes to visualising how their home might look wallpapered or with a new sofa or curtains. But we'd no plans for a shop or a showroom. We'd assumed our little self-built website would be enough of a selling platform. Budgets were starting to run dry, and we ran the risk of all our efforts and costs being in vain. So, we looked around us and realised that we had a space all along – the Hackney house that had been the catalyst to start the brand. So, we decided to turn it into our showroom. It was all smoke and mirrors. We could only afford to dress three rooms, each styled in one of our debut collections. The front of the house with its grander rooms and high ceilings became the stage for photoshoots and appointments. The back rooms remained unchanged – white and drab and strictly off limits – a quiet reminder of how tight things really were. When we launched, the press loved the fact that the House of Hackney was a real house. They found it conceptual. In truth, it was just a necessity masquerading as vision.

In 2010, the high street still reigned supreme, and the market was flooded with cheap, disposable product. We were designing an aesthetic that was quintessentially British. For reasons of authenticity, craftsmanship and a desire to support British industry, we knew we wanted to make the product in England. But would we still find factories willing and able to craft the products of our dreams? Had they survived the onslaught of the high street? We didn't know.

As total newcomers to the industry, we didn't have a little black book of suppliers. So, we embarked on a six-month road trip, driving around the UK in our van on a mission to find factories to produce our designs, our one-year-old son strapped to us. The leads didn't come easily, but as we travelled the length and breadth of the country in our trusty VW Transporter, we were heartened to find pockets of localised industry that still existed – small, generational factories in historic manufacturing areas where skills continued to be passed down through families.

Though orderbooks had shrunk due to the dominance of the Far East-produced, high-street trends, the machines were still rolling. We found heritage fabric mills in Lancashire, wallpaper and furniture in Loughborough, ceramics in Stoke-on-Trent, carpet in Devon and textile weaving in Suffolk, whose roots stretched back to the silk weavers of Spitalfields near our East London home. I'm forever grateful to these heritage manufacturers who took a punt on a young couple with a little blonde-curled toddler in tow and a big dream to put the spotlight back on UK craftsmanship. Many of the artisanal factories we met on that fateful journey remain our partners to this day. We've slowly grown together, through relationships that transcend the transactional and are rooted instead in trust, respect, and genuine care and friendship.

We called upon our creative friends, photographers and stylists like Celestine Cooney, David Dunan, Kimi O'Neill and Suzanne Beirne, who were used to producing high-concept fashion editorial. They offered their time, talent and generosity, pushing our ideas further, stretching our shoestring budget and helping alchemise the spirit of the brand into a visual identity. They were the first people to see and feel the ranges. Their excitement, and early personal orders for their own homes, gave us a first flicker of hope that maybe others would feel it too. Their belief in us carried us through the many moments of pre-launch self-doubt when we couldn't help but wonder, were we on the right track?

We scraped across the finish line with a massive sense of relief at the end of those nine months. With stoic tenacity, creativity and a little help from our friends, we'd somehow managed to navigate the tight budgets and still deliver a vision and product that we were proud of and which honoured the ethos of our early vision. Things were finally falling into place. All the ingredients seemed to be there for a successful launch.

In the lead-up, we hosted back-to-back press interviews at our house, gently ushering editors into the front rooms only, hoping to preserve the spell and keep the illusion intact. There was a genuine buzz about it. The press had never seen anything quite like it. In a landscape where safe, identikit interiors had long dominated, here was something unapologetically bold, imaginative and on its own terms. They jumped on it, captivated by this new vision of interiors, and the coverage was wild – we featured in all the publications of our dreams.

The April 2011 launch of House of Hackney was a technicolour landing in a sea of beige. We had blown the last of our budget on an ambitious pop-up: a takeover of a three-storey townhouse in the heart of Dalston, wrapping it in our Dalston Rose collection and transforming it into a topsy-turvy art installation, where furniture hung from the ceiling and every room showcased the bold, fantastical universe of House of Hackney.

Set against the hauntingly ethereal soundscape of the music of Zola Jesus, it was an utterly sublime experience for the senses. The launch party was hosted by a then-rising actress named Gwendoline Christie who, in a twist of fate, had found my dropped passport on the street and traced it back to our front door. Over cups of tea in our kitchen when she graciously returned it, we bonded over our shared season of uncertain but hopeful beginnings. I showed her the sketches for our soon-to-launch brand and, by the time she left, she had offered to host the party.

The morning after the party, nursing heavy heads and a sense of relief that we'd made it, albeit with some scars to show for it, we logged onto the website to check our first orders. A big fat zero. Was the site working? We ran test orders. It was. A sinking dread began to creep in.

We had been naive. Coming from Topshop, where launches sold out instantly with press fanfare, we expected some commercial traction. But here we were, totally new to the interiors scene, offering an aesthetic that was so radically different it could have come from Mars and at a price point many weren't used to, especially in the economic aftermath of a recession.

We soon learned that interiors were a different kind of purchase. People needed time to shop interiors. They ordered wallpaper samples and taped them to their walls. It was often a collective decision. They got their partner's buy-in. They slept on it. The decision process could take a lot of time. But we didn't have months.

The real fight only began after the launch when we had to pedal so hard just to survive. The hard work we could handle, but it was the persistent dread that lived in the pit of our stomachs that truly tested us. In those first few months, and well into the first year, the colour drained from everything. I was ashen-faced, caught in a near-constant state of fear and shock. Javvy became a husk of himself. We were gripped by panic. What the hell had we done? We felt reckless, naive, foolish even, for leaving our secure jobs to chase a dream. What did we even know about the business of interiors?

We withdrew from friends and kept our distance from family as I avoided the usual weekly calls home for as long as I could get away with. The sound of my father's kind voice would have undone me completely. So, I consciously kept him far from our struggles, preferring to carry the burden privately, too ashamed to admit how bad it was; how wrong we had got it.

By then, we had two young children to look after, and we were surviving hand to mouth. For the first time in my privileged life, I had a taste of what poverty feels like. I learned that the cheapest food is usually the most processed. That it's hard to eat healthily when you're broke. I vividly remember being at a friend's house and being served berries in abundance – and thinking how lucky they were to be able to afford to feed their children berries, and how far we had fallen. Sundays were often spent doing local car boot sales just to afford lunch – a far cry from the days when our only concern was where to go for brunch. That first Christmas was impossibly bleak, improved only by a lovely friend loaning us their Christmas tree while they were away. There would have been none otherwise. During those dark days, the clarity of our vision faded into the background. I learned that survival mode leaves little room for idealism. Conversations about sustainability or impact felt like a privilege we couldn't afford when all we could focus on was trying to keep our little family going.

Javvy was on the verge of taking an evening job in our local pub when, finally, the tide seemed to turn. But it began with a false dawn. Selfridges came knocking, offering us a shop-in-shop, with just thirty days to design and produce the space. It sounded like the answer to our prayers – we desperately needed visibility. We scrambled to meet the deadline, working round the clock with our factories. But two weeks before the deadline, they pulled the plug – there had been a change in buyer and a new direction. Just like that, it was cut. It felt like the final nail in the coffin. When I put the phone down, I collapsed in a heap on the showroom bed that we couldn't sell and sobbed.

We were out of energy, out of ideas, out of hope. We'd poured every-thing into this, every ounce of ourselves, and now we were just shadows, hollowed out by the effort and haunted by the thought that we'd made a terrible mistake. But that day, I learned that a brutal morning could sometimes bring a golden evening. That afternoon, I dragged myself out of bed for a long-planned *Guardian* interview and photoshoot, too broken to even cancel it. My eyes were red-rimmed from crying, visible to all the readers. Well, maybe just to me. But when the feature ran, a beautiful editorial on our story and mission, there came a shift. Perhaps readers resonated with what we were building and saw the realness etched across my face in the photograph. Whatever it was, the orders began to trickle in. At first, it was just £2 samples of fabric and wallpaper. We noticed it was the creative directors and the bolder interior designers who came first – those confident in their convictions.

Build it and they will come. And gradually they came. The dread began to lift with every order, every kind word, every message of thanks for the joy House of Hackney was bringing. They recognised the beauty. And it buoyed us to keep going. We knew in our hearts that we weren't designing for everyone. We were creating for the ones who really feel. For those who see the soul in a print; the poetry in a pattern; the story in a room; the wonder in the natural world.

CHAPTER 7

The Roots of Company

'To nourish with beauty at the table of life.'
Steve Corcoran (1986–2023)

In his book, and a personal bible, *Radical Love*, the activist, wisdom keeper and my friend Satish Kumar traces the word company back to its Latin origin, *companio*, meaning 'a group of people who share bread together'. It speaks to companionship, fellowship and a gathering bound by common intent. A company wasn't about business or transactional relationships – it was rooted in the principles of connection, trust and survival. To break bread with someone was to forge a bond and sustain one another. Before companies became boardrooms and balance sheets, they incorporated friendship, loyalty and shared purpose. Even now, beneath the corporate veneer, the etymological meaning lost to bottom lines, it's an undeniable truth that a company is only as strong as the people gathered around its table.

I like to think we subconsciously tried to honour that spirit from the very start of House of Hackney. At first, House of Hackney was just me and Javvy, and we wore every hat in the company, from design to customer service to dispatch to bouncing the baby. It was solid teamwork, but also a crash course in business operations. Then came Kirstie. I don't think we would have got very far without her. She was part of a group of cool Hackney girls who worked at our launch weekend Dalston pop-up shop. In the chaos, when we were pulling all-nighters on the installation, with no time to even assign any kind of roles and responsibilities, Kirstie instinctively stepped up and took the reins. Although her only job up to that point had been working in a pub, she had a natural flair and a quiet fierceness as she brought a sense of calm and order to the madness. A stickler for process and perfection, she turned out to be a total natural at operations.

We instinctively looked after Kirstie – and those who came after her – like family. Even though we could barely feed our own, we'd cook lunch every day for the team. Over those first few years, we must have baked thousands of jacket potatoes, warming both the house and our tummies, when we could hardly afford to heat the place, as a token of appreciation for the all-in commitment it took to sustain a start-up in those early days.

Although today it's a bigger family, it's still very much a family – and Javvy and I continue to honour the ritual of cooking lunch for the team. It's something we do to mark each season – spring, summer, autumn and winter – and to celebrate the unique bounty each one brings. The ingredients are usually picked from our garden in Cornwall, then cooked and served as a simple act of gratitude for those who give so much to the brand. Outside of these seasonal gatherings, we come together twice a month to share lunch, stepping away from our desks to, metaphorically, break the bread that is at the heart of 'company'. We place an almost spiritual value on sharing food that's been grown with love and cooked with consciousness and which hums with vitality, seeing it as a life-giving force, a delicious gift from Nature's own supermarket, nourishing and healing us. And it's a chance to gather, a sacred pause to connect with one another on a deeply human level. It's the spirit of company we're committed to keeping strong.

The pressure of that first year was enormous. We were trying to keep our heads above water, to feed our little family, to keep everything, and everyone, going. I had even been asked by a male shareholder in the early days to promise that I wouldn't get pregnant in those first years.

But then Lila appeared, making her presence known through the lessons she was trying to teach me before I even knew of her prenatal existence. She reawakened in me the knowledge that my purpose wasn't out there to be discovered, but inside me to be remembered.

Like many Indigenous cultures, I believe that far beyond what is perceived as the irrational whims of the pregnant body is actually a heightened sensitivity that carries with it a kind of deep ancestral wisdom and intuition; a sense of what nourishes it, what protects it and what to turn away from. It's instinct in its most unfiltered form, guiding not just for survival, but for sacred preservation. If we allow ourselves to listen to it.

My daughter, growing inside me, was the first to truly show me what my body had long been trying to say: that my 'always-on' mode of technology, the glow of screens and the invisible frequencies were making me sick. The moment I opened my laptop, a wave of nausea would rise, sudden and visceral, as though my body were recoiling from something it could no longer ignore.

The emissions, which pre-pregnancy would make me feel like I had a bit of a hangover when I overworked myself, now felt toxic and unnatural. 'Mum, put your tech down and get outside,' she insisted to me in utero.

My body was calling me into something deeper. It was waking me up to the profound difference between fingers pressed into living soil, like my farming grandmother did every day even when with child, and my fingers tapping endlessly on plastic keys. One reawakened my biology through its contact with microbes, boosting my mood and immunity; the other overrode my nervous system, flooding it with cortisol, heightening anxiety and fracturing my attention.

The only place I could muster short thirty-minute bursts on my laptop was outside. I'd slip off my shoes and sit in our tiny garden, feet pressed to the earth, cupping ginger tea in my hands and the breath of the outdoors gently retuning my nervous system like a soothing balm. Nature recalibrated me and counteracted the digital drain.

This was the beginning of my setting up of little outdoor offices, a practice I've done since anywhere I could plonk a table just big enough for my laptop and a cup. If it wasn't raining, I'd take every chance to work outside, chasing the sun until it dropped behind the neighbour's wall, stretching the seasons as far as I could. In winter, I'd bundle up in layers of wool, fingerless gloves, double-socked in my Uggs with a hot water bottle tucked under my coat. Once April came, I'd swap them for my battered Mexican sun hat, bare feet kissing the ground, gradually peeling off layers until the sun dropped and it was time again to cloak up.

It's a paradox not lost on me that as someone who has a company built around interiors, albeit one where we bring Nature into the home, my favourite room has come to be the garden. I dream of living outside... of us all living under the sky. Of creating beautiful outdoor rooms that fit form to function and withstand the elements, where we can spend most of the year living outside, reclaiming that aliveness that is waiting to be activated beyond walls and screens. Perhaps my body remembers on a visceral level a time not so long ago, thirty years or so, when my life was lived more outdoors than now. Or perhaps the remembering runs deeper in my very cells along ancestral lines. Working outside in Nature was about as close as I could get in my urban life to the kind of rude health my grandparents had from working the land.

I could feel a real difference in my level of aliveness when I worked outdoors – a new vitality that stirred in me, like my creative antenna had been switched on again. Later, I would discover the science that backed up what my body already knew: that exposure to natural light and contact with soil and plants supports our circadian rhythms, harmonises our day and seasonal cycles, sharpens our creativity and activates our gut biome as it boosts our immunity and soothes our frazzled nervous systems. Time in Nature heals and enhances us.

———

By the end of our first year, we'd run out of space and had to close the public front door of the house and break down the showrooms. The only trace of those original collections was the wallpaper on the walls. Our home then became HQ: a design studio, a warehouse, a functioning office, all squeezed in alongside a growing family. We were bursting at the seams. Even getting the larger orders down the narrow staircases and out the front door for the DHL driver became a daily logistical nightmare.

As the sample orders gradually turned into real orders, the business began to stabilise and we could finally see a future beyond just the next month. Our creative mojo returned after a spell of paralysis – and with it, we picked back up the big dreams. We started to allow our minds to wander, imagining the full universe of House of Hackney. If we had a shop, what would it look like? Where would it be? What would it feel like? What would it smell like? Although we weren't out of the woods yet, the signs were beginning to show that the nascent company had legs. Liberty, our first stockist, was starting to sell the brand well. I can still remember Ed Burstell, the managing director at the time, palpably excited as he called House of Hackney 'Liberty's little sister'. It seemed that where there was customer traffic, and people could see, touch and feel the product – and get some personal assistance – it sold. We also knew, from the sweet messages our rare customers sent when they received their orders and waxed lyrical about the quality and attention to detail, that the website didn't do the product justice. It couldn't fully capture the quality or convey the emotion of what we were creating.

And in our imagination, we held a world much bigger than what a screen could convey. We dreamed of a space where customers could step inside the world of House of Hackney – where they could see the prints at full scale, hear the soundtrack that inspired the collections, feel the textures, and be completely immersed in the universe we were building. Our work/living setup was becoming increasingly unsustainable – the mix of growing children and start-up under one roof was far from ideal. Yes, it was time to start looking for a space of our own.

From the first meeting with a local estate agent, we learned that for a business at our stage and size, securing a retail space would require a hefty upfront deposit – close to a year's rent – and when we factored in the cost of fitting it out, it became clear that our own shop was off the cards unless we found some investment. Serendipitously, a private investor, who had been working with Hackney Council on regenerating the area, crossed our path at a party. Jack understood Hackney, loved it and had a background in luxury heritage retail. He saw the same potential in us that he saw in the borough. He believed in what we were building, and we saw in his mentoring presence a palpable excitement for our vision.

Jack really got it, and with his background and gentle temperament was a great fit for us. He, alongside his business partner, Adam, liked what we were doing, and they were happy to support us on our journey and at a pace we were comfortable with – no pressure was applied to accelerate growth, to achieve higher margins, to swap our factories and British craftmanship for Far Eastern iterations. They backed our ethos of small production runs of products that were made to last in heritage factories. We agreed on a cheque size that we were both happy with for a minority share in return. This investment became the key that unlocked our next chapter: a proper shop, a real office, stock to fill the shelves and the ability to invest in a small team to help run it all. Jack, during his time with us, was a dream investor, cheerleading us through every high and low with the unconditional love of a parent, opening his little black book of contacts, opening doors to luxury department store buyers who ended up becoming stockists and making introductions to seasoned luxury brand CEOs to help us on our journey.

Two years after our launch – in April 2013 – we opened our first store on Shoreditch High Street. At the time, it felt like the coolest high street in the world – one that bucked the onslaught of homogenisation and was alive with independents and a raw kind of creativity. We'd visited countless shops across Hackney, but one by one they fell short – too rustic, too polished, too cramped, too clinical, too hidden. Then, one day, just as we were close to parking our dream, we asked on the off chance about a storefront on the high street where building works had been going on for months, which was rumoured to be the site of a new Prada store. The rumours didn't surprise us. Although still a compared to Central London, the area felt like the electric epicentre of everything. This part of Shoreditch High Street, butted up against Redchurch Street and Calvert Avenue, felt like a little slice of New York's East Village in London. The agent said he'd check – and lo and behold, it had just become available.

On paper, it was a cavernous shop housed within an imposing four-storey Victorian stuccoed building with a penthouse – with only a small, chocolate-box window at the front to cast light into the space. Inside, it was stark – dank and grey, with poured concrete floors, exposed grey frieze blocks, and a brutalist winding staircase that led to a dark subterranean basement that ran the length of the shop. But we weren't deterred. What others likely saw as unfinished, we saw as a space we could truly make our mark on. And as a bonus, there was a floor of office space directly above the shop that was also going. The size and location felt perfect, and we knew we could transform this blank canvas into something special.

The story of Biba, the legendary 1960s and 70s London fashion brand founded by the visionary Barbara Hulanicki that revolutionised retail with its theatrical stores, had transfixed me ever since I was given a shiny black-and-gold coffee-table book in my early twenties. It stirred in me a longing for a time I hadn't lived through but desperately wanted to experience – a moment when a shop wasn't just a place to buy things, but a portal into another world. A universe where you could step inside and find your people but also lose yourself in. Barbara Hulanicki's vision of retail – how she completely turned the shopping experience on its head – and the iconic world of Biba she created blew my mind. Especially the Kensington High Street shop with its legendary Rainbow Room: all black lacquer, leopard print and printed paisley velvets – like my granny's home on acid. It was decadent, immersive and unlike anything London (or I) had ever seen.

That level of theatre stayed with me. Biba wasn't just a shop, it was a world. Escapist, seductive and completely transportive. It turned shopping into storytelling. Our first flagship had to be more than a shop. We wanted to create a world – a place where people could step inside and really *feel* something. Where they would resonate emotively with the space: feel awe, curiosity, inspiration. Where every product told a story, where the shop tellers were storytellers, and where nothing was purely transactional but relational too. A shop that wasn't just about selling but about belonging.

We handed that Biba book, alongside one on Hackney's original Victorian hothouse, Loddiges, to MRA Architects when they asked to see our inspiration for the Shoreditch High Street store. They had designed some of our favourite retail spaces, and we knew they were the ones to help bring our vision to life. They were as kind as they were visionary. Not only did they design our dream shop, but they took a chance on us and let us pay them in shares, becoming early board members. And so, out of the raw, cave-like interiors, we created our own kind of Gothic indoor garden rooted in the sense of enchantment and an irreverence that was already in our DNA. We laid Victorian black-and-white chequerboard tiles underfoot, installed lacquered midnight cabinetry that made the prints pop and bounced off the mirror-panelled octagonal ceiling. We filled the space with trailing ferns and towering palms. It felt part Victorian conservatory, part enchanted den of iniquity. And it seamlessly looked like it had always been there.

On our opening day, Barbara Hulanicki was the first person through the doors – a pinch-me, full-circle moment. With the warmth of someone who had walked the path before us, she shared her wisdom around staying true to our vision and empathised with how hard that early stage of business and life was. Our story took her back to being part of a young couple with young children, birthing new creative worlds of their own.

The shop ushered in a golden era for the brand as it really put us on the map. Later that first year, *Time Out* would vote it the third-best store in London, after only Selfridges and Liberty. What made the shop truly magical, though, was the feeling it gave. I loved hearing the first gasps of people as they pushed open the heavy brass doors and passed through the dark velvet Palmeral entrance curtains – the threshold into our House of Hackney world. It hit them immediately: the sensory beauty, the tactility, the sounds and music. It stirred something deep, moving them in ways they didn't expect. People found it intoxicating – and they came back, day after day, just to feel it again. We finally had a space where human interaction could thrive and, very quickly, the shop became a neighbourhood institution, a hub that buzzed with life, brimming with customers all seeking something colourful and storied.

The locals were brilliant: maverick artists, designers, stylists, creatives, still very much living in the area in those days, not yet swept away by the tide of homogenisation that would creep in over the following years.* We wanted people to be able to save up and invest in a piece that was truly special – designed with purpose and made with love.

---

* The area would eventually be swallowed by developers and global chains looking to capitalise on its cool factor; our beautiful store, stripped of its spirit, would become a Starbucks.

Inspired by William Morris, we shared his belief that design should be democratic and accessible, enjoyed by all – not just an exclusive few. So, we made a conscious decision from the start: although the quality was luxury, we'd work to lower-than-usual profit margins and pitch an accessible luxury price point, so more people could enjoy these pieces in their homes. Beyond the usual metrics of success, we placed a big value on our factories having orders running through them, the workers being paid fairly and this income supporting the flourishing of the local communities. Especially in those early days, when the high street reigned and products were cheap and disposable, we had to gently educate our customers on the idea of buying less but buying better and that our prices were the real cost of manufacturing in the UK.

The press called us the New Maximalists, and we were credited with launching an era of aesthetic maximalism, but it was a label we were never entirely comfortable with. More was more when it came to colour, pattern and spirit, but less was definitely more when it came to consumption. It wasn't about having lots of stuff. There was a widespread expectation of low retail prices, shaped by a market fuelled by the high street's mass production. We had to shift that mindset – to help people recognise the value in pieces made with care, by skilled hands, in fair working conditions, using beautiful materials that were built to last.

We wanted people to invest in fewer, more meaningful pieces that would last a lifetime. We saw our sales team as storytellers, and they played a vital role in this, guiding customers through the journey of each product, from its inspiration in Nature to the craftsmanship behind its making. They helped people see it not just as an object, but as the final expression of a thoughtful, intentional cycle.

———

In the first few months of the shop being open, I'd often work Saturdays, quietly dusting the navy panelling up a ladder, covering lunch breaks and helping as we found our feet with operations. Over the course of a few weekends, I noticed the familiar sound of an Irish accent. I soon came to recognise a beautiful, impeccably dressed young

Irish man who would glide into the shop, giving his visiting friends warm, passionate tours of the space – with the inner knowledge of a museum guide. He spoke about the brand and our collections with such insight and heart that it stopped me in my tracks. Without even asking for a CV, I offered him a job.

Steve very quickly became the heart and soul and face of House of Hackney. It turned out that he was fashion trained: a gifted designer who could turn those golden hands of his to anything – clothing, interiors, tablescapes, floristry – always leaving a trail of breathtaking beauty in his wake. He was, in so many ways, the embodiment of everything we stood for: his aesthetic, his creative flair, his culturedness, and his emphasis on fun, friendship and family.

In our world of interiors, he had an intuitive gift for reading people's tastes and dreams, turning their ideas into rooms that felt like home to them; and in the process, forging friendships that lasted far beyond the design.

But what stood out most was not just his talent but his way of relating. Relationships were at the heart of Steve's values. He ripped up the rulebook that called for distance between designer and client, employer and employee, manager and report. Instead, he brought everyone close, creating a deep sense of family. We encouraged this transcendence of the usual constructs of relationship because I had seen at Dunnes how hierarchy fosters walls and distance. Steve showed us the opposite: how collapsing those barriers created belonging, trust and the roots of a different kind of company.

Steve had an incredible gift for spotting new talent. Over the years he brought so many exceptional people into the fold, taking his mentoring of the new recruits very seriously, investing emotionally and nurturing them with such patience, care and pride. Nothing made him happier than seeing them flourish.

Just over a decade after he first walked through our doors, we lost Steve suddenly in the summer of 2024, under unfathomably sad circumstances. His passing shook the very core of House of Hackney like nothing else ever has. The grief felt impossibly insurmountable. After our share of company low points over the years, this was the one moment where Javvy and I weren't sure if we could really go on. But we came to realise that it's the pact that we make when we open our hearts to love our people deeply.

At a team away day a year before his passing, in the gardens of Trematon, we workshopped through our individual purpose as a fun self-discovery piece, and so that we could understand and honour each other's true self at work. At the end of the day, Steve read out his personal purpose statement: *To nourish with beauty at the table of life*. I don't think he realised that in those words, and all he stood for, the real roots of company were alive and present.

Steve lived his life in service of beauty, making the worlds he touched infinitely more magical, expressive and emotive than he found them. Now, on the wall by our meeting rooms hangs a banner made from the fabric of his favourite print, Plantasia, with the words *Be more Steve* sewn on. It's a daily reminder to all of us to put people first, to love without fear, and to find the awesome beauty in the everyday.

CHAPTER 8

The Money Tree

'In nature's economy … the currency is not money, it is life.'
Vandana Shiva, *Earth Democracy*

B y Year 4, we were facing some serious growing pains. It was a real inflection point. From the outside, it looked like everything was coming up roses. The brand had grown by word of mouth, the most authentic type of growth, and by now we were being shopped by a dream roster of customers – creatives we revered, musicians we adored, actors we'd grown up watching and of course our brilliant locals. Our wallpapers were now hanging in the kind of rooms we'd only ever dreamed of. People from all over the world, seekers of spirit and Nature lovers were making pilgrimages to our flagship looking to be inspired by this new universe.

We never had the budget to advertise, nor did we feel inclined to even if we had. We were happy to be this strange little dream on the liminal edges of the interiors world. What began as a peripheral brand with a cult following of the creatively curious and quietly rebellious, shopped by those in the know (if you knew, you knew), started to resonate far wider, reaching people we had never imagined, but who were also looking to be moved and inspired.

We'd always hoped House of Hackney would be ageless and genre-defying, and now we were seeing this in real time, with even the City boys in suits, spilling out from the big banks just a stone's throw away, wandering in on their lunch breaks, flat whites in hand, fawning over floral wallpaper. It's funny that they were unknowingly brushing up against the very thing their world was designed to ignore – Nature. I'm not sure entirely how I felt about it, but the genie was well and truly out of the bottle. People fell in love with the prints – wild, untethered, surreal expressions of Nature – that spoke a different language to each person, eliciting deep emotional responses: of awe, of love, of memory. What fascinated us was how different designs resonated with different people, each one unlocking a feeling entirely their own. There was a kind of psychology to it all that the team became deeply attuned to. Like intuitive alchemists, they learned to match people to their prints, sensing their moods and colour needs often before the person even knew themselves.

But having a shop stretched us thin. We suddenly had a big space to fill – and felt the pressure to respond to every customer request: I'd love this print on… a notebook, a washbag, a teacup, a soap dish. Not everyone was ready to invest in interiors or had the budget, so the smaller, pick-up items became a way for people to take home a little piece of the brand. And slowly, almost without realising, we found ourselves offering as many product categories as a department store like Liberty. Our made-to-order model was now sitting alongside ranges that required high minimums – and those minimums began to gobble up our cash.

We even ended up dipping our toes back into fashion, something we'd once sworn we left behind in our past lives. These capsule collections for men and women were at least made in England by small-scale factories who manufactured for heritage British brands. But while they were brilliantly received and opened doors to new customers, new markets and exciting collaborations, fashion turned out to be a cash-intensive beast. With high production costs, minimum orders and super-slim margins, it quickly became more of a drain than a driver.

Around this time, the luxury department stores who had been circling us came calling to place wholesale orders and offer spaces – big global names like Lane Crawford, Neiman Marcus, Bergdorf Goodman, Harrods and, of course, Liberty. On paper, these were exciting opportunities and the chance to get more eyes on the brand was important. But the reality was more complicated. The wholesale model was tough: low margins, high stock commitments and sometimes a sale-or-return basis that meant the risk sat squarely with us. The message was often that we should do it for the visibility. But visibility doesn't pay staff wages or keep the lights on. For young, independent brands like ours, the wholesale model can be a brutal setup. Javvy and I were still carrying what I can only describe as a kind of lingering PTSD from those early years, never quite sure if we were going to make it, always braced for it all to implode at any given moment. It's a feeling that still creeps back into my tummy at the faintest whiff of a downturn even now, tightening like a muscle memory. So, we said yes to everything that might futureproof us. Everything, that is, except the high-street collaborations we turned down, proposals that, on paper, would have solved our financial worries overnight. But we had to decline. Because they went against the very fabric of values and purpose that House of Hackney stood for.

We'd never had deep-enough pockets and were still running on the fumes of small friends-and-family EIS investments, along with Jack and Adam's more significant contribution, which was tied up in buildings. Our board meetings back then were quite the spectacle. A true motley crew of the auntie, who kept interrupting just to say how fiercely proud she was, old-time raver friends turning up straight from the club, our architects and builders, whom we'd gifted shares to as a thank you for helping us build the business, literally, and Jack and Adam, who patiently humoured the chaos while Javvy and I did our best to keep things vaguely on track. At least we had strong month-on-month sales figures to report!

But with the responsibility of expensive rent, bigger production runs for wholesale partners and long payment terms, often stretched even further to 60, 90, even 120 days, we were getting into deep water. From the outside, it looked like we were flying. Inside, we were more exposed than ever. Our overheads had skyrocketed. We now had a scarily high fixed-cost base: a flagship store, offices and a growing team of around twenty people, all of whom depended on us to pay their rent and mortgages. The retailers were hungry for orders and the customers were lining up, but the weight of the buildings, the people, the tight margins and those brutal payment terms was crushing us. What had started as a dream to creatively sustain our little family was morphing into a much bigger beast. And with that came the pressure, the responsibility, to protect and provide for this expanded family.

To make matters worse, we had a famously strict landlord. If rent was even a few days late, he'd send bailiffs to the store: heavy-set men who stood at the entrance, intimidating our team. It was absolutely mortifying. We found ourselves relying on short-term, high-interest cash loans, even putting our house up as collateral. We still weren't paying ourselves a liveable wage and our household income was so far under the threshold that the only silver lining was that our toddlers qualified for free nursery care – at a loving, local community nursery that quickly became an extension of our family. Without family close by, I honestly don't know how we could have functioned as parents, as partners or as co-founders without that support. We were exhausted. Burned out from being in survival mode and running on cortisol and adrenaline for so long that although there was such brand love, the financial pressure felt insurmountable. The increased demand, while flattering, was slowly killing the business.

It was a customer who first mooted the idea of private equity (PE) when he popped into our shop. It was the era, in the mid-2010s, when PE deals were happening everywhere in fashion. From the outside, it looked like the ultimate seal of approval. And from where we stood, drowning in financial stress, it felt like a lifeline – a way to finally feel secure and park the perpetual fear of doom we couldn't shift.

We bought into the idea that it would safeguard the brand, take our relentless money worries off the table and allow us to bring in a senior management team to help shoulder the load. We weren't totally naive about the model – we'd seen what happened to mission-led brands under private equity. We saw the sad demise of the beloved Body Shop, once Anita Roddick's ethical beauty pioneer, as it was sold to corporate giants and later passed between PE owners, eventually gutted and pushed into administration.

And Laura Ashley, whose floral textiles had adorned our homes and mothers' dresses in the 1980s, fell under debt-fuelled buyouts, management churn and rapid expansion, only to collapse into administration and become just a licensed name. Even Toms Shoes, a real pioneer for business as a force for good, the poster child of social enterprise with its one-for-one giving model, buckled under Bain Capital's ownership, ending in a debt-for-equity swap that wiped out the control of its founder and diluted its original mission. And Ben & Jerry's ice cream, despite legal safeguards when it was sold to Unilever, has faced ongoing tension as corporate priorities clash with the brand's outspoken social activism, culminating in the resignation of co-founder Jerry Greenfield in 2025 after he complained that Unilever had moved to silence its stance on Gaza. Again and again, it was the same pattern of the original purpose being diluted and the founders sidelined in the pursuit of profit. We were determined: that wasn't going to be us.

But somehow, those warnings didn't come through from the charismatic consultant we paid a lot of money to advise us, who dazzled us with possibilities. And so began a six-month parade in front of the big private equity firms. We were trotted out like show ponies to the fancy offices of the big PE firms and spent months pitching the vision to people so far removed from our aesthetic and mission, and many really not getting it, not understanding what we saw in beautifully unruly Hackney.

Eventually, a deal was presented. On paper, it looked like a great fit. Values-wise, it felt like the best match, and we genuinely admired the cohort of brands the firm had invested in, many of which were aligned with our own ethos. We were elated and deeply relieved. The prolonged and costly quest to find a private equity partner had finally paid off. All the time, energy and money we'd poured into the process had been worth it.

And then it fell through. I'll never forget the day that we got the news. It was Javvy's birthday – a day that began with the brightness of a new chapter of a secure future on the horizon. But by the afternoon, the wind had been knocked clean out of our sails.

It wasn't long before the chairman who'd been proposed in the previous deal came calling. We were the ones who got away, he said. He was excited by the brand's potential and if he could find the right deal for us, would we still be open to it? In the aftermath of the deal falling through, a lot of people told us that we'd had a lucky escape.

But we needed to get to a place of safety quickly or else there would be no House of Hackney. We were drowning in pressure – cashflow, overheads, responsibilities. So, when the opportunity of private equity came round again, it felt like the lifeboat we'd been waiting for. And, either way, we didn't have an option if the business was going to survive its current cost base. The alternative would have been to let go of the team and shop and offices and, mindful of the work family that we loved and supported, this was the last thing we were prepared to do.

Javvy and I felt confident we could structure a deal where we were protected; insured against any of the horror stories we'd heard about founders losing control. Staying in the majority was essential to this. Majority shareholders had the power, and we knew it was the only way to safeguard the heart of the business to ensure we retained both creative freedom and strategic direction. We believed that if we held over 50 per cent, we could steer the ship. The cautionary tales, tragic stories of founders who lost control of their brands, who watched their visions diluted or dismantled – that wasn't going to be us. It was a majority deal, or no deal at all. This was non-negotiable. But we were about to learn just how slippery control can be.

Private equity, we came to learn, is a little like a political party. It swoops in with bold promises offering the dream of growth, support and stability, but often the model is built on a short-term tenure, financial wins and a maximum return on investment, at the expense of the long-term consequences of those decisions. With private equity, the day they sell is as important as the day they invest – it's all about the exit and their return on investment. What happens after that is not their problem. There's rarely a commitment to the long arc of a brand's journey, nor much care for the people who built it, the purpose behind it or what would be left behind once the profits were extracted. Once the numbers are up and the value mined, the story ends there for them.

But true governance, whether in business or politics, doesn't just think about the next quarterly report or election cycle. It builds for the next generation. And this was my and Javvy's mindset, even if we did not yet have the future generations' language for it at the time. We weren't building House of Hackney for a quick flip or a short-term return. It was not just our brand, but a collective one – and our role was to safeguard it. We had no planned exit strategy. We were building and caretaking for the long haul, and for a legacy beyond our own tenure. This wasn't just a business to us; it was a living, breathing system, created to nurture craftsmanship, support meaningful employment and cultivate joy and lasting beauty inspired by the natural world in the most sacred space of our lives – our home. Our margins existed to sustain local factories, not to be squeezed for shareholder gain. We made our philosophy clear from the outset: if a potential partner was aligned with our purpose and our trajectory, and was happy to commit to a minority shareholding, then, and only then, would we move forwards.

Eventually, a deal was proposed: a partnership with a relatively new private equity firm who, by that stage, had a few deals under their belt. The valuation was one we were happy with in exchange for a significant minority stake. It wasn't a controlling share, so we, as majority shareholders, would retain the power to continue steering the company's trajectory. As an added bonus, they described their approach as 'hands off': monthly board meetings and regular reporting, but otherwise we'd be left to run the business as we always had. It sounded ideal. Even their name had a benign, Nature-based quality to it that, coupled with charming personalities, gave the impression of alignment and suggested a promising foundation for partnership. I've learned since that the language of Nature is often co-opted to mask an agenda that's anything but Nature-honouring. From Amazon to Nestlé, BlackRock to Blue Origin, we've seen how the names and language of Nature are borrowed to hide the sharp edges of extraction.

We passed all the usual stages of their due diligence. We presented ourselves as we were: hard working, committed and values led. Our five-year plan was laid out in detail; our forecasts rigorously stress-tested. Together, we spent months modelling the next three to five years and collaboratively agreeing on how we would allocate the seven-figure investment to fund the infrastructure needed for the next chapter: across stock, systems, a senior management team. And finally, after five years of living hand to mouth, a provision for salaries for ourselves. The deal was as good as done. Contracts were drawn up. We had begun to build the senior team, offering roles under the promise of this new chapter. Suppliers were firing up the factories, ready to fulfil the orders our customers were waiting for.

From spending time with us, the investment firm started to realise something we'd never hidden but perhaps they'd never truly grasped – that we really hadn't founded House of Hackney to build it up and sell it. That we didn't have a five-year countdown for an exit strategy to cash out and walk away. Analysts of the private equity sector have observed that the model is typically designed to maximise value and achieve an exit – often within three to five years – rather than to nurture a brand for the long term.

A majority control typically allows investors to dictate the terms of that exit – when, how and to whom – with only limited interference from the founder. Industry analysts often point out that when a founder holds the majority stake, the exit process runs the risk of becoming slow and unpredictable and valuations can become harder to realise. Founders are usually more emotionally and creatively invested in their brand, which can make them hesitant to sell and resistant to changes that maximise short-term value but risk diluting their founding vision. From the perspective of an investment firm, it is preferable to have a controlling stake in the business.

At the eleventh hour, the day before we were due to sign the deal and officially become partners, we were called into an impromptu meeting at a London hotel with the PE firm and our newly appointed chairman, the guy who had brought the deal together. We were told that the company would require more cash – a few hundred thousand more to be precise. At first, I didn't fully grasp it. A little more money? We had spent countless hours with these same people poring over cashflow projections and capital requirements. Every sales scenario – good, bad and ugly – had been modelled and stress-tested. The investment already on the table was far from insignificant. The cheque was sizable, with a healthy balance of working capital earmarked to see us through. Our sales forecasts were steady, slower than what might thrill a PE firm, but an intentional growth plan all the same. There were no immediate plans for new store openings or major expansions. To us, after our months together of meticulous planning, it was difficult to comprehend why this request was surfacing at this late stage.

The explanation we were given was that this was about 'protecting the company', ensuring we had sufficient buffer for success. It was presented as if it were a minor tweak, a prudent safeguard that any sensible founder might accept. But as I listened, I began to run the numbers in my head, and it became clear that even a relatively small increase would tip their shareholding past 50 per cent, shifting us from majority owners to minority stakeholders.

I gently pushed back, trying to steady my trembling voice as the bottom felt like it was falling out of our world again, and asked why this was surfacing at such a late stage. What I remember most was a line offered with warmth, but which landed heavily with me – that it might be 'better to hold a smaller stake in a successful company than a larger one in a struggling business'. The words were delivered in a way that felt friendly on the surface, yet to me carried the weight of an ultimatum.

It felt like a decisive shift in power. The last-minute request, presented as protection, would in practice rewrite the entire foundation of the partnership. Still, although wide-eyed at the exchange, we tried to stay calm in the moment. There was too much at stake not to. On the surface, the offer sounded reasonable, but its ramifications were seismic. The proposed cash injection was significant enough to take us from 52 per cent to below 50 – it threatened to undo everything we'd built.

Javvy, ever trusting, began to articulate his thoughts on giving them the benefit of the doubt – that perhaps it was a last-minute oversight. I understood the impulse. These investors had been presenting themselves as partners, even mentors, for months. 'OK, let's pull back on some spending to make the numbers work,' I offered. But that wasn't taken up as an option. What was put forward felt non-negotiable: either we accepted the new terms or there would be no deal. In that moment, it struck me that we had little real choice. The timing, the delivery and the way this extra cash happened to shift the balance of power all felt, to me, to be uncomfortably pointed.

My inner voice, which had guided me through so many tough calls, was telling me to hold my ground, even as the conversation weighed heavily and our world seemed to be crashing down around us once more.

We carried a responsibility – not just to ourselves but to everyone who depended on the company. To cave now would feel like a betrayal of everything we'd built. 'I'm sorry, but no,' I said quietly but firmly. Javvy looked at me wide-eyed; I could sense his palpable concern, knowing the deal would probably now unravel and the consequences we would then face. Across the table, the mood shifted almost imperceptibly. Javvy backed me, still visibly shaken, but steady enough to add that the new request felt too different from what we had originally understood. 'We'd prefer to walk away than agree to these terms.'

Later, I came to understand that what we encountered resembled a common feature of some private equity negotiations: once founders are fully committed, new terms may be introduced that shift the balance of power. In our case, just as we were preparing to walk away, a different option was suggested. The head of investment proposed including a covenant in the contract: if the business failed to hit certain year-on-year growth targets over an agreed timeframe, they would be entitled to invest more money at the same pre-money valuation. In plain terms, that meant if growth slowed, they could put in additional capital at today's price rather than a potentially higher future valuation. The effect of such a clause could end up increasing their ownership at more favourable terms if performance faltered. Even though, if triggered, it could move us into the minority, it initially seemed a highly unlikely scenario. We had grown month-on-month, year-on-year since launch, and with new investment fuelling stock and infrastructure, we believed the trajectory could only continue upward.

The clause was set to track success metrics over a two-year period with quarterly reviews, comparing each year's trading and profitability to the previous year. It sounded reasonable at the time, and the likelihood of breaching it felt very remote. What we didn't fully appreciate was – and our advisers didn't flag – how it actually could play out in practice. Because once we began spending the investment as planned, hiring senior leadership, building stock, upgrading systems, our EBITDA (earnings before interest, taxes, depreciation and amortisation) was bound to dip in the short term compared with the leaner previous year. EBITDA is the standard measure of profitability – sales less the operating costs. Ours would naturally drop, not because the business was failing, but because of the investment phase itself. Even with stronger sales, that temporary dip could trigger the clause. Later, I came to learn that this kind of provision is often referred to as a ratchet mechanism. It can function as a way for investors to increase their ownership if growth targets aren't met, sometimes shifting majority control. Critics of private equity note that such clauses can be particularly challenging for founder-led, purpose-driven businesses, where growth may be steadier and less exit-focused. Framed as risk management, it can still feel like a trapdoor for founders.

———

It was April and time for a new innings. Everything significant always seemed to happen to us in that month. We were looking to the future, feeling a deep sense of relief that we'd finally reached the safety we'd been running towards for so long. That this deal would stabilise the brand and allow it to fulfil its beautiful potential. There would be gas in the tank again – stock levels replenished, our energy restored. And after five years of living hand to mouth, we would finally be on a salary. We even booked our first holiday in years – a week in Cornwall in July. It felt symbolic. Finally, a moment to breathe, to pause and not worry. Javvy had always wanted to take me and the kids to Cornwall. Just having a holiday on the horizon felt like light at the end of the tunnel.

Behind the scenes, we got down to work with renewed vigour. For the first time, we were able to build out a proper senior leadership team – a real dream team of mostly working mums, all brilliantly experienced and emotionally intelligent women. At the helm was Sam, our new general manager, formerly head of merchandising at Liberty. Whip-smart, capable and clear-sighted, with buckets of emotional empathy, Sam became our company anchor. She brought the operational and financial rigour that Javvy and I had been missing. Sam steadied the ship. She introduced structure and process, streamlined our product offering by cutting what no longer served and overhauled our backend systems. She also transitioned us to a smarter operating model, shifting 75 per cent of our goods to made-to-order and implementing drop shipping, freeing up cash, and stock and reducing our footprint.

We never set out to build a team that was largely female and LGBTQ+, but in hindsight, perhaps subconsciously, I was trying to recreate the sisterhood I'd known during my Topshop days. I'd grown up in matriarchal Ireland, where women often held the reins of family, business and community, leading not through dominance but through empathy, resilience and a soft power. It wasn't a matriarchy in the formal sense, as patriarchy still shaped the institutions, but women were at the helm of every home, holding it all together. These roots ran deep from the time of the Brehon laws, when women held rights to property, leadership and even divorce, long before most of Europe. The spirit of Brigid, the goddess and the saint, was prevalent not just a relic of the past, but as a living force that subconsciously still moved through generations of Irish women as they personified power that doesn't reside in force or fear, but in intuition, renewal and the ability to create and nurture lasting change.

While British society was built on conquest, hierarchy and a male dominance, Ireland has somehow retained a more fluid, community-rooted and female-centred resilience. I grew up with role models like Mary Robinson as our president. Mary was the true definition of a stateswoman: dignified, principled and softly radical. She showed us that you could lead with heart and still change the world. And maybe it was also a quiet response to the men who had used power not to protect but to possess, from the predatory advances so many of us endured as young women, to those in positions of authority who wielded it carelessly, or worse. That's not to say I haven't had beautiful men in my life: my husband, my father, my closest male friends, my team members – men full of humility, compassion and care. But still, I think I had always instinctively recoiled from a certain kind of dominating masculine energy (and it's not only men who carry it), the kind fuelled by ego, hierarchy and control – where money is equated with power and success with domination. We still have a prevalence of this energy today: tech billionaires and political strongmen who genuinely believe they're entitled to shape the world in their image. That old model of masculinity – extractive, performative, disconnected – just never resonated with me. We were drawn instead to creating a team and culture that was softer, more emotionally intelligent, more cyclical and intuitive.

The one position the private equity partners emphasised was head of finance. They regarded it as essential and, because finance was their area of expertise, we assumed they knew what 'good' looked like. The chairman would lead the hiring process, and we deferred to his judgment. These were both new dynamics for us. In principle, the role of a chairman is meant to be that of an impartial steward – someone who supports both founder and investor, bridging financial strategy with values, vision and long-term legacy. Over time, however, we sometimes found ourselves questioning whether that balance was being maintained. At first, we wondered if it was simply our own intuition. But gradually, we felt less certain, and began reflecting on how competing interests can make true impartiality difficult.

And this, I think, is where governance in early stage investment often falters. The structures are primarily designed to protect capital and minimise investor risk, but rarely to safeguard the brand or the people who built it. That imbalance can leave gaps in accountability.

For the head of finance role, we were introduced to an ambitious young candidate – confident, personable and with solid references. The investment firm, along with the chairman, strongly backed his appointment. Finance had always been our least confident area. We were more financially literate than many creative founders – in the early days we made it our business to stay close to the numbers, forecasting sales, forensically checking VAT returns, knowing our margins down to the decimal. But we weren't accountants. And once we began outsourcing financial management to external specialists, we became aware of how vulnerable that reliance could make us.

That July, the children ran barefoot through the orchard of the little cottage we'd rented in Cornwall, our laughter carried on the sea air. We were so happy. Three months into the deal, we had just closed our first financial quarter. Sales were strong. To our eyes, everything seemed to be going to plan. And then the call came.

It was the head of finance. The tone was formal and a little apologetic. 'I'm sorry to interrupt your holiday but I have some bad news. You've breached the covenant criteria.'

My blood ran cold. It had to be a mistake. Sales were strong, the board meetings had all been positive. 'No,' he said. 'I'm afraid you've failed it.' And so, the clause was explained again, and the penny dropped. Our fleeting taste of freedom immediately evaporated. What had seemed like the beginning of a new chapter instead exposed vulnerabilities built into the deal. Beyond the devastating impact on our ownership was a deeper, more unsettling truth that this was not the kind of partnership we thought we had entered.

What struck me most was how unmoved they seemed. Neither the head of finance nor the chairman gave any indication that they had considered the personal impact on us as founders. Their response was that we had signed the agreement, and it must now be honoured. What made it even harder was later discovering, to our surprise, that the head of finance had been offered share incentives during his time with us. From our perspective, this shifted the dynamics in ways that left us questioning where loyalties lay.

And just like that, the clause could be triggered. The so-called subscription criteria could come into effect, the additional investment would be released and, with it, our majority shareholding would dissolve. For us, this marked the beginning of the darkest chapter in House of Hackney's story. The next two years felt like an unrelenting period of pressure coinciding with the ticking timeframe of the covenant, leaving us feeling increasingly worn down.

I began receiving Friday night phone calls from the lead investor. From my perspective, these calls felt strategically timed, just as weekends began. They would leave me unsettled during what was precious time with my children and I would end up carrying the weight of the conversation for the whole weekend. Though framed as prudent advice, I experienced the message as a form of pressure: that there was no way out, that the covenant breach was final, and that we had to accept it.

Impromptu board meetings, from our perspective, began to feel less like open discussions and more like pre-prepared presentations. These took place in the glass box of our boardroom, with the chairman showing PowerPoints that emphasised the company's urgent need for more cash and outlined what we might stand to lose if we didn't agree, including our home. Close to breaking point from the pressure, tears would roll down my face, visible to the team passing by.

To us, these sessions felt one-sided, more like presentations aimed at steering us towards certain outcomes than any kind of open dialogue. They were delivered with such conviction that it often left us questioning our own judgment and doubting ourselves. The more we pushed back, the more we felt destabilised and unsure of our footing, while the terms we thought we had agreed to seemed to be shifting.

To make matters worse, our house had been used as security against a business loan. Any wrong move, and we stood to lose not just the company but our home.

I understood that their ultimate objective was likely a clean exit, but I couldn't fathom what seemed to me the short-sightedness of the approach. Without us, House of Hackney would not have been what it was. We *were* the brand, and we held the relationships on which everything built – our team, our suppliers, our customers were all loyal to *us*. Working *with* us would have produced the best outcome for everyone involved.

It was our bank, in the end, that made us look twice at what was happening. Our manager called us to their office out of concern. They'd reviewed recent trading figures and forecasts and were worried about our financial performance. We were confused. Sales had been strong. Nothing on our end suggested a problem.

During that conversation, the bank manager raised questions about the forecasts they had been shown, which, from their perspective, appeared unusually conservative. It was suggested to us that, if taken at face value, such projections might discourage the bank from extending any further finance. Hearing this was the moment the veil lifted for us. We realised that things might not be as we had assumed, and that we needed to act carefully.

A couple of days later, I happened to overhear a phone call between some of the parties in our office corridor. The tone and content struck me as reinforcement of my growing fears that interests inside the business were becoming closely aligned in ways we had not anticipated. In that moment, my stomach dropped.

It felt chilling to imagine how far things might go and how coordinated it all seemed, at least from my vantage point. Yet, in a strange way, it was also clarifying. With that realisation, the fear began to recede, and I began to fight back with all the power I had.

The head of finance and the chairman stepped down with the changes taking immediate effect. After that, the investment firm, perhaps concerned about its own position, became much less active until the covenant's ticking two-year timeframe finally expired. We had come so close to losing everything we had built, and, in my view, it was only by holding the line that we survived it. I could just about hold it together through board meetings, but I could no longer look our partners in the eye. For Javvy and me, the trust we once had felt shattered – completely and irreversibly.

And yet, throughout it all, we never once reneged on our duties as directors. We drove the business to meet its targets. We continued to lead the team with inspiration and care, showing up to every single board meeting with utter professionalism, even when we found ourselves sitting across the table from people whose approach felt, to us, increasingly adversarial. What kept us going was the unwavering light and energy of our team, who showed their love, loyalty and belief through even the darkest days. Together, we kept the business going and growing. Despite feeling under intense pressure from our investors, the numbers spoke for themselves. Month after month, we as a team were delivering.

It wasn't until 2023, seven years into the investment partnership, that we finally felt our energy and confidence begin to rise again. After a few years of countryside healing, we had slowly pieced ourselves back together. For a long time, we'd been too wounded to act, too exhausted, and we felt too paralysed by the pressures of those years to think about doing anything about it. But one morning in early January, after a restorative Christmas break, I woke with complete clarity. It was time.

The weight of what we'd endured became impossible to ignore. At times, the experience felt almost torturous, leaving us drained and destabilised, with outcomes so destructive in their potential that we could barely fathom them. Had we not fought tooth and nail to protect what we had built – the business, our home, our family life – we might have lost it all. There is no doubt in my and Javvy's minds that without that resolve, House of Hackney as we know it would no longer be alive today.

I knew then that we couldn't stay silent – not for us, and not for the next founder who might unknowingly step into the same kind of situation. I resolved that our story would not end in silence.

When we never received the apology or closure we hoped for, there was no option left but to bring in lawyers to represent us. For a long time, I doubted I had it in me, but when the moment came, the lioness in me roared again. In the end, the legal process itself became a form of leverage, leading to a reduced company valuation, which, with the support of a crowdfund and B Corp bank Triodos, enabled us to buy it back and become House of Hackney's sole gatekeepers once again.

Never again would we hand the soul of what we built to anyone who might see it only as a transaction. Never again would we allow House of Hackney's purpose to be compromised. That purpose, rooted in regeneration, beauty and service to life, is now written into the company's Articles of Association. In black and white, our objects are defined as not only to promote the success of the company for the benefit of its members but also to:

Have a positive impact on Nature, minimising the prospect of any harmful impact of the business and its operations on Nature, and having due regard for the interests of Future Generations. Article 2.1(b–c)

And, crucially, no single stakeholder interest can outweigh another. As our Articles state:

For the purposes of a Director's duty to act ... a Director shall not be required to regard the benefit of any particular Stakeholder Interest or group of Stakeholder Interests as more important than any other. Article 2.4

This balance is at the heart of our mission: ensuring that decisions are not made at the expense of Nature, people or future generations, but in service of all. By locking the company's mission into law, it means that our purpose is no longer just a statement of intent but legally enshrined. It ensures that, regardless of who owns or leads the business in the future, House of Hackney's commitment to regeneration, people and planet cannot be watered down or abandoned. So that everyone who comes after us will be bound to honour it. So that the spirit of the company can't be diluted, sold off or steered away from why it was created in the first place.

The real win for us wasn't ownership. The victory was reclaiming its purpose and ensuring it could be protected and fulfilled. Now, we had the freedom to do just that.

Freedom to return to the roots, to the very foundations of the House.

Freedom to redefine what 'success' and a successful company should really mean. Not the biggest, not the fastest, not the most performative, but the one that delivers on these deeper responsibilities.

Freedom to reimagine business not as a machine for endless growth in a finite world, but as a living organism, capable of playing a major role in healing, contributing to and regenerating our communities and ecosystems.

Freedom from the extractive metrics of profit and growth tied to the traditional investment finance model and its expectations. We now had the opportunity to create a business model, one that would integrate with Nature, one that aligns with life.

Because just as GDP is a broken measure of national progress, so, too, is profit a dangerously narrow lens when it becomes the sole measure of a business's success.

It tells us nothing of how that profit was made.

It doesn't ask whether it came at the cost of forests, rivers or communities.

It doesn't care if it sacrifices wellbeing, creativity or future generations along the way.

It's a system that has short-sightedly forgotten, in the words of conservationist David R. Brower, that 'there is no business on a dead planet'.

For too long, investment finance has misunderstood how a money tree works, treating companies as if they are resources to be stripped, flipped and exhausted for short-term gain. It forgets that businesses, like Nature, are living systems made up of people, relationships, creativity and care.

Finance would do well to remember that companies flourish when their roots are nourished, when their branches are supported and when the ecosystem around it is allowed to thrive. Because, like Nature, abundance flows when these conditions for flourishing are in place.

CHAPTER 9

Trematonia

'Tell me, what is it you plan to do
with your one wild and precious life?'

Mary Oliver, 'The Summer Day'

'Last night I dreamt I went to Manderley...'

Cornwall had been in my dreams since I was fifteen, when my mum passed me her old musty copy of Daphne du Maurier's *Rebecca* like a rite of passage; it had been her favourite book as a teen, and it soon became mine.

I was completely intoxicated by the story and the relationships within, and by Rebecca, the De Winters and Mrs Danvers. But most of all, I was captivated by the hypnotic Manderley estate and the novel's broader setting of a place called Cornwall, with its hidden coves and ever-changing seas. How could a place exist where palm trees kissed hydrangeas and rolling hills met turquoise waters, all set against a backdrop of myth and magic? Javvy had spent long teenage summers chasing waves and girls on the north coast of Cornwall. For as long as I'd known him, he'd been trying to take me there, but life kept getting in the way. It took me almost twenty years to finally make it. And it didn't disappoint.

That first summer after our private equity deal went through, when we could finally allow ourselves a little holiday, we packed up the car and set off on what would become an annual escape to Cornwall. As we drove over the Tamar Bridge, it felt like we were crossing into another country. Here was a land left to its own untethered beauty, far removed from the halls of power in London and our own life responsibilities. Although it was my first time setting foot in Cornwall, it felt like a homecoming. There was something deeply familiar about the rugged landscapes of moors and sea, the Celtic spiral stones and the spirit and warmth of the people who welcomed us there. I suppose it was a living reminder that Ireland and Cornwall were once part of the same landmass – and were still infinitely connected.

We would arrive in Cornwall shells of ourselves, overworked, carrying heavy tech hangovers, worn thin from the psychological toll of our investors and feeling very Nature-depleted. Those carefree, sun-drenched summer days became a time to refill our cups in Nature. We would wake in our tent to birdsong, wash in the azure waters of secret beaches beyond the reach of Wi-Fi and enjoy the momentary precious disconnection from being always on.

We camped in wild, tucked-away places that led to beaches accessible only by the coastal path, the sea reviving us each morning before we set out to explore hidden coves and Cornwall's famed subtropical gardens. As part of our immersive exploration of this corner of the county, we'd often visit the odd house for sale, pipe-dreaming about what it might be like to live this way all year round. Cornwall was a healing balm for us – a place where we could stitch ourselves back together and remember who we were and that what we most deeply needed was simple time in Nature, together.

We would time our annual pilgrimage to Cornwall to coincide with the Port Eliot Festival, a place where writers, musicians, artists and dreamers gathered in the spirit of pure, unfiltered creativity. The date became a permanent fixture on our calendar and one of the main highlights of our year. It refilled our cups with an intoxicating dose of creative stimuli – the setting, the characters and the programming all contributed to an alchemical melting pot that kept us nourished long after the tents were packed away.

The combination of time in Nature and a glut of inspiration would power us through the months ahead, just about sustaining us until July came around again. We'd leave Cornwall with heads full of inspiration, with new colour palettes picked from the gardens we'd wandered through and matched to our Pantone book, new ideas sparked by the festival's magic and a fresh wave of creative themes waiting to be explored in our work. To be able to pour into the House of Hackney, we first had to refill ourselves.

London had given us the community and convenience we needed to keep going. It takes a village, and we were lucky to have a wonderful one on our doorstep, holding us closely as we juggled the nascent baby stages of family and business. But with every visit to Cornwall, it became more and more clear that without a deep immersion in Nature, something vital was missing in our life. Nature didn't just restore us, She sharpened us, made us better designers and more intuitive decision-makers. The more time we spent in Nature, the more our sense of wonder was reawakened.

On that fateful summer trip, I reread *Rebecca* for the first time since I was a teenager. Reading it in du Maurier country, it felt as though I had stepped into its pages. As the sea crashed against the cliffs and the smell of rhododendrons hung in the air, I could literally close my eyes and taste Manderley. That holiday we visited Trebah House and Gardens, with its uncanny resemblance to it – both houses perched on hillsides with hidden pathways and gently sloping gardens where untamed Nature spilled towards the sea. It felt like fiction had blended into real life. At night, Manderley permeated my dreams.

I was accustomed to that bluesy feeling that came with leaving Cornwall, like slipping out of a dream you didn't want to wake from. The solemn journey home was always the antithesis of the ebullient road trip there. As we drove along the A38, bound for London, the car packed to the rafters with camping paraphernalia, I spotted a brown-and-white heritage sign – the kind my eyes had become trained to notice by now – that marked a place of history and culture.

It read: Trematon Castle Gardens.

This place had lived in me long before I ever saw the sign. Its famously enchanting gardens, planted by the royal landscape gardening alchemists Isabel and Julian Bannerman, had held a kind of mythical status in my mind. 'Stop!' I shrilled. Trematon Castle Gardens had been buried deep on my Cornwall bucket list for years.

'No more gardens!!' came the groaning chorus from husband and kids. But, somehow, I got my way. I can't remember how exactly. I may have bribed them with the promise of cake in a castle. What I do remember is that within ten minutes we were parked in the farmer's field that served as the summer car park and the kids had already forgotten their resistance .They roly-polied down the hillside, the long grass cushioning their falls, as we made our way to the entrance of the castle walls of Trematon, a gateway to another world. We were met with a gruff welcome from Julian, who was tending to a patch of acanthus and informed us it was 'cash only', which, of course, we didn't have on us. But after a chat about William Morris and his love of acanthus, he waved us through with a jolly 'Have fun!'

This was early August, and the orchard hung heavy with apples, plums and a generous old mulberry tree. Everything here seemed supersized – giant, ancient holm oaks held court, their sprawling limbs heavy with centuries of wisdom, while medieval gunnera, with leaves the size of small boats that looked straight out of Jurassic Park, rose like prehistoric sentinels. The softness of Nature was constantly juxtaposed with the stone medieval gatehouse and castellated perimeter walls, which deftly held the many worlds inside together like the walls of an old theatre containing a thousand unfolding acts.

We lost and then found six-year-old Lila, dancing wildly through the sprinklers, her joy so unfiltered as it mirrored the untamed energy of the land around her. The hunt for her broke the entrancement with the mundane reminder that we needed to hit the road. And so, reluctantly, we began the long drive back to real life. How lucky were the Bannermans to inhabit a world like Trematon's.

That night as I fell asleep reading *Rebecca*, Trematon and Manderley seemed to merge in my dreams, my subconscious picking up their synergies, both perched above the sea and steeped in atmosphere and spirit.

What happened next will give me goosebumps forever.

A couple of nights later, back in London and already settled into our routines, I got a call out of the blue from Andrew, an estate agent we'd met on one of our speculative house views.

He beat around the bush for a while; talking about how he knew how much we loved Cornwall, how he'd had lunch with some friends on Saturday, and how they were thinking about moving on from their place, how it was becoming too much for them. Would now, perhaps, be the right time for us for something in Cornwall? Whatever he was trying to pitch didn't sound especially compelling.

'Well, Andrew,' I said. 'We've only just got back. Shame we missed seeing this. Where are you talking about?'

'It's a place called Trematon Castle,' Andrew said. 'Have you heard of it?'

Had we heard of it!

He went on to describe how he'd been there on Saturday, the very same day we had. As we wandered the gardens, lost in the beauty of the place, he was in the kitchen having tea with the Bannermans. Telling them about a young couple from Hackney who loved this pocket of Cornwall.

We both nearly fell off our chairs.

The main house had been off limits to garden visitors, so we'd only admired it from the lookout window of the gatehouse; peering up at its elegant Georgian symmetry and floor-to-ceiling windows, wistfully imagining what it might be like to live in this enchanting place.

'So… What did you think?' he asked.

Without missing a beat, without saying that I needed to consult my other half on this huge life proposal, without even asking to take a closer look at the house, I instantly said: 'Yes.'

'Well, this was just a casual round-the-kitchen-table conversation,' Andrew said. 'I'll need to check if they're definitely serious about moving.'

And they were.

This was a summons to a place, if ever I understood one. Although we were ready to say yes based on the gardens alone, the Bannermans insisted we visit the house, just to be sure. The main Georgian residence had been built in 1808 from the stones of the old castle wall, which had been knocked down to open the sweeping estuary view that the house faced. Adding to the growing list of coincidences, this work had been carried out by the tenant at the time, Benjamin Tucker, who is an ancestor of Javvy's best friends from childhood, Matt and Richard Tucker. The stuccoed villa itself had a beautiful symmetry to it, designed in the neo-classicist style of Sir John Soane and constructed around a central atrium. Trematon was about five times the size of our house in Hackney, yet, somehow, its proportions made it feel cosy and lived in.

We used the visit to take measurements, knowing it would likely be our last time inside before the move we hoped to make in the new year. Julian took us around the garden, as we frantically tapped notes on the flora and fauna into our phones. What began as a tour became, in essence, our handover. The meandering path down to the estuary, he told us, was affectionately called Manderley Drive!

After what felt like a divine calling to take it on, came the reality: the practicalities of making it happen. Trematon was a leasehold property under the Duchy of Cornwall, operating on a twenty-year lease – not the easiest arrangement to secure a mortgage for. The two-decade lease wasn't for everyone. No one could take it to the grave. But then no one takes anything with them, anyway. There was no passing it down. No guarantee that the love and investment we poured into it would ever yield a financial return on our exit.

But Javvy and I were already well-versed in the value of looking after something for the joy, the experience, the fulfilment and the purpose of the journey itself – all the markers of a life well lived, as we saw it. We had no interest in obsessing over an exit plan, a sale or a final return on investment. Just as we felt about House of Hackney, regardless of what was written on paper, we instinctively understood that no one truly owned Trematon. No one, that is, apart from Nature herself. Instead, we saw it as a profound honour to hold a tenure there, even for a relatively short chapter, as its caretakers. I use that word deliberately, because we weren't gatekeepers guarding a treasure, we were there to care for it, to have a relationship with it. Our role wasn't to preserve Trematon unchanged, but to be in service to its needs during our time there, to tend to them lovingly and possibly for it to shape us in return. We saw value in the immeasurable, life-affirming experience of this unexpected chapter in our family's story, in listening to the land, learning from it and immersing ourselves in its wild, untethered spirit.

———

To secure a mortgage on our new home, we needed to release our London house as security against a business loan and transfer it instead to our shareholding. This was 2019 when House of Hackney was still part-owned by the PE firm, and even though it would have had little impact on our private equity partners, we needed their written permission. Although we were investment 'partners' with near-equal shareholding, the business debt at that point sat solely on our shoulders.

In that vulnerable moment, when we were already far into the process, we were presented with terms we had not expected: in exchange for agreeing to release the security, they asked us to sign an agreement giving them greater control over a potential future sale of the business. For us, this felt like déjà vu – a replay of the high-pressure situations we had already experienced. Once again, it felt as though we were being pushed into a corner.

We had already paid the deposit on our new home, packed up the house and given notice to the children's schools. There were tenants lined up for our London place, the children had said goodbyes to their friends and we had mounting pressure from our vendors' solicitors, who were threatening tens of thousands of pounds of daily penalty fees if we missed the completion date. Against this backdrop, the demand landed like a blow. From our perspective, our most vulnerable position had become leverage in negotiations, leaving us facing another impossible choice: the company or a new chapter for our family. I felt defeated. It felt as though they finally had us.

By now, we should have been settling into our new life in Cornwall, all timed so we could set up home before the children started the summer term at their new school. Instead, Javvy loaded up the car and drove the children to the southwest, slowly inching towards Cornwall. They stayed in B&Bs, spending days on the beaches of Devon, trying to kill time, as he tried to create some sense of normality for them.

I remained in London, trying to unlock a solution. For three weeks, I spent sleepless nights on a sofa in the office, homeless and beside myself with fear about the consequences of the situation. The only person I confided in was Juni, our cleaner. Every night, as she emptied the bins and wiped down desks, she'd find me on the sofa in a state of paralysis. She would kneel beside me and whisper, 'It's going to be alright,' her soothing Jamaican voice the only thing holding me together. But at the time, I struggled to believe it.

Bone-weary and empty of ideas, I felt backed into a corner and on the verge of surrender. And then, as we came within a hair's breadth of the completion deadline, a voice inside reminded me of something simple but powerful: the reputation of a private equity firm is its life-blood. Money follows trust. And if there was even a whisper of doubt around their reputation, it could jeopardise future deals. No founder in their right mind would partner with them if they knew how this felt from our side. So, I drafted an email to the most senior director, explaining our experience and indicating that we would feel compelled to share it publicly if we couldn't resolve the situation. It wasn't something I took lightly, nor something I was comfortable doing, but by then it felt like our only choice.

I never received a response from him. But not long after, an email landed from our investment lead agreeing to move the security. The gates finally unlocked.

I raced to Paddington, jumped on a train to Cornwall and went straight to a local solicitor's office. We completed the deal with just twenty minutes to spare. A few months later, after making our move so difficult, the partners suggested rolling our new home, Trematon, into the wider group under the rationale of 'increased buying power' – a proposal that, from our perspective, would have served primarily to lift their exit valuation. For us, it was a chilling reminder of how differently we saw the business and its assets.

After the bleak weeks of camping out in the office as I tried to unlock our future, London was still stripped bare by winter, spring's green cloak not yet arrived. I couldn't even allow myself to visualise what Trematon looked like; at this stage, it was feeling too much like a foolish dream that we'd read too much into. But as we drove through its curvy wrought-iron gates on that unforgettable April day, we gasped out loud at the sheer beauty that confronted us – made even more breathtaking by the long and bruising road it had taken to get to this place. Trematon in spring was nothing short of an earthly Eden; soft lilacs, vivid purples, creamy whites and a parade of yellow daffodils in seemingly infinite variety against a backdrop of birdsong.

It was straight out of a Disney film. Heaven on Earth. Thank God we hadn't given up.

When we opened the curtains that first morning, we were greeted by a view so dreamlike that it hardly felt real: a viaduct built by Isambard Kingdom Brunel spanning the horizon, a twin of the viaduct shared with our beloved Port Eliot further down the estuary, its slender train track sashaying gracefully over the water. With a low mist hovering above the river's edge, catching the morning light, it looked unreal – like a living model railway.

But it's the smells that bring me back to our arrival at Trematon year after year – the honeyed drift of jasmine from the orangery, the sharp green punch of wild garlic carpeting the woods and the powdery, nostalgic scent of lilac filling the orchard. Lila's birthday fell the day after we arrived that first year. When we named her, we had no idea that lilacs would blossom, faithfully, each year in the weeks around her birth. We had dragged the children kicking and screaming from London to cries of, 'We don't want more Nature!' A few days later, they started at the local primary school – and never looked back.

Trematon quickly became a gathering ground for our tribe of friends and family – a kind of blissful commune where we sprawled across generations. From new babies to grandparents, we shared long, spiritually nourishing days filled with food, music and play. Guitars by the fire. Big communal meals. Raucous football matches on the lawn. Dancing late into the night.

For that first blissful summer, we turned a blind eye to the fact that once it had been emptied the house itself was in a total state of disrepair, far worse than we'd anticipated. The windows were rotting; just restoring those alone would take the best part of a year. Friends who visited us in those early days tried to hide the anxiety they had for us even though it was etched on their faces, the sheer scale of the labour ahead impossible to miss. We probably seemed naive. But this part didn't scare us. Not after everything we'd been through. When our furniture finally arrived from storage, it filled only about a fifth of the house. We prioritised fixing up the gate lodge and the cabin in the woods to get some income to help Trematon begin to wash its own face.

The garden had been left to fend for itself while the sale was going through, and Nature had quickly begun to reclaim it. We weren't given a manual for Trematon and our experience with gardening extended only to a few hopeful potted plants in our tiny Hackney backyard. But we were hungry to learn. That was why we were here – to get an education in Nature. We began to slowly explore and observe the garden, walking its paths like students entering a new school. I'd always known Javvy had green fingers, and I was especially excited for this chapter, for him to develop these skills and knowledge further.

In London, as he lovingly tended to his potted tomatoes, learning to nurture them and ward off pests, Javvy had already begun to look into the harmful effects of Roundup and glyphosate on soil degradation, biodiversity loss and their link to cancers. He started to really question these dominant gardening practices that treated Nature as the enemy: casting weeds as threats to the aesthetic, depicting insects as pests and wildness as something to be tamed, forgetting that each plays its own vital role in Nature's ecosystems. Javvy was becoming deeply curious about how to garden *with* Nature, not against Her.

Soon after, he signed up for a permaculture course at the Apricot Centre in Totnes so that he could learn how to work in true synergy with the land and its cycles, rather than try to control it. We had inherited an ornamentally beautiful garden; a real showpiece of planting where each riot of flowers gave way to the next in a seamless, sublime reveal through the seasons. But our dream was to cultivate something deeper than the surface-level aesthetics – a garden that was so rich in its biodiversity, alive with pollinators and teeming with all the conditions that allow life to truly thrive there. Javvy began following the work of regenerative growers like Charles Dowding and other no-dig pioneers, drawn to their ethos of working with, not against, Nature.

All the while, the ticking of the twenty-year lease reminded us that this dream was bound by time. Trematon taught us that true stewardship is not about owning or controlling, but about listening, intuiting and co-creating – serving the spirit of a place (or a company) and its deeper purpose. Our role was not to preserve but to serve, and to let the land shape us in return.

And so, the real purpose of our time at Trematon started to reveal itself. It was becoming clear that we weren't there to just restore a house or reimagine a garden, but to build a deeper relationship with Nature. The more we observed, the more we immersed ourselves and the more we began to understand how Nature operates: in cycles, in shared exchange, in right relationship. We saw how Nature gives exactly what's needed, when it's needed. We saw how nothing is wasted, how everything is interconnected, with every part playing its role in service of the whole. How there is no competition, just cooperation. No short-term grabs, just long-term balance. Nature doesn't force growth; it creates the right conditions for its emergence.

It was the healing power of Nature in its most potent effect. It resuscitated us and, though we did not yet have the language of regeneration, we were being shown a glimpse of another way – a way beyond the extractive logic of conventional business. It reminded us that if we want anything to truly thrive, whether a garden, a company or its culture, we need to start by sowing the right conditions for life, not through force or control, but through deep trust, care and relationship.

That it wasn't about chasing outcomes at all, but about creating environments in which the right outcomes can unfold. And slowly, the downloads of enquiry started to come.

What if companies were also modelled on Nature?

What if they were set up with the right conditions for flourishing? With the right relationships, rhythms, reciprocity and regenerative systems? Surely, they would thrive too.

And what if we modelled our company on Nature's perfect living systems? We were beginning to hypothesise that, just like the garden we were in, the healthiest, most resilient organisations grow when they are held by systems that are cyclical, transparent and adaptive.

Trematon was already planting the seed that the future of our company might just lie in remembering how life itself works.

Perhaps the most radical blueprint for business was the one Nature has been offering all along.

CHAPTER 10

Small Is Beautiful

*'Modern man does not experience himself as a part of nature
but as an outside force destined to dominate and conquer it. …
Forgetting that, if he won the battle, he would find himself on
the losing side.'*

E.F. Schumacher, *Small Is Beautiful*

'It takes a year to begin healing a field,' said our new neighbours, Tim and Claire Williams, regenerative farmers, aka land healers who, like us, had recently arrived on the southwestern peninsula we were both now calling home, drawn here by the call to restore what had been neglected. They had been invited to revive the land of a nearby estate by a landowner who'd heard Tim speak at a farming convention about the practice of regenerative agriculture – an ancient-but-new way of working with the land that came with the remarkable upsides of healthier soil, greater biodiversity, and a way of farming that could actually restore more than it takes.

The Tamar Valley, where we now found ourselves living, had once been one of the most fertile agricultural regions in the UK, a patchwork of orchards, market gardens and small-scale farms before decades of intensive industrial agriculture leached the soil's nutrients and exhausted its land. Now our new neighbours had been called in to begin the work of bringing it back to life.

By then, we were about six months into our own journey at Trematon, and already we were beginning to witness Nature's bounce-back.

After just one year without pesticides or synthetic fertilisers, the changes were undeniable.

One of the first jobs Javvy undertook was to install a natural pond, designed to restore a missing freshwater habitat and create a corridor for amphibians, insects and birds. Before long, grass snakes began appearing, drawn by the re-emergence of life at the water's edge. We also began introducing a wider range of native plants, chosen for their ability to thrive in succession and flower throughout the year, creating more stable, resilient habitats for Nature.

It was the pollinators we noticed first as they started to arrive in their droves: bees burrowing deep into the foxgloves in search of nectar, hoverflies whirring like miniature helicopters and a kaleidoscope of butterflies in such abundance that I couldn't always identify them – peacocks, red admirals, the occasional painted lady and countless more. I remember the reports of the dramatic decline of butterfly sightings in the news that summer raising alarm bells for biodiversity. And yet, at Trematon, we were witnessing a reverse trend. It seemed that all that was needed were the right conditions to thrive, and life would return in its abundance.

We started to notice the changes in the soil as it began to darken and grow rich with worms and the delicate lacework of fungal threads. Wildflowers started to appear even without our planting as they naturalised on their own, spreading a delicate layer of colour and scent over what had previously been scutch grass. The garden that was once more manicured and controlled felt like it was beginning to finally breathe again as it became more and more alive. Yes, from what was unfolding, it did seem entirely believable to us that Nature could begin to heal in just a year. Tim and Claire affirmed what we were witnessing: that life wants to bounce back and flourish when it's given the right conditions.

It was exciting to learn about regenerative farming – a system that felt like not just a soil revolution but a soul revolution, too. It was a return to relationship, to reciprocity, to remembering our place within the web of life, where life is supported and not diminished. And unlike industrial agriculture, which depletes the land year after year until it can no longer support life, this approach did the opposite. It healed. It enriched the soil, restored biodiversity, supported pollinators and even helped draw carbon out of the atmosphere to then sequester it back into the ground.

We learned that in complete contrast to conventional agriculture – with its heavy reliance on synthetic fertilisers and tilling, which releases stored carbon and becomes a net emitter of greenhouse gases – regenerative farms could act as carbon sinks. Regenerative agriculture not only offered a pathway to ecological repair but had the potential to be one of the most powerful tools we have in the face of climate change.

With all the climate fear swirling around us, it was honestly such a relief to hear something hopeful. That we do have solutions. That the land wants to recover. That Nature, given half the chance, wants to thrive. And that it wasn't about forcing growth or squeezing the most from the land but about creating the conditions for life to flourish and abundance would follow. To do that, we need to let go of so much of what we'd been taught to celebrate as 'progress': our obsession with yield, the dependence on chemicals, the urge to dominate Nature rather than work with Her.

These ideas came truly alive around the Sunday lunch table, often over roast lamb that had been reared on the very land we were learning about. It was Tim who first helped me understand the essential role animals play in the regenerative farming cycle. He explained how, when managed properly, grazing animals don't need to be extractive but can actually become restorative, helping to fertilise the soil, stimulate plant growth and build biodiversity. After almost a decade of vegetarianism, his perspective gently challenged much of what I thought I knew. Slowly, I began to embrace a little of what was naturally part of the system: animals that had lived within the cycle, that had contributed to the health of the land and, in doing so, offered their nourishment to us in return.

My original reason for giving up meat had been to honour Nature's sentience. In sort of the same way, I never liked picking flowers, preferring to let them stay in the soil with their flower families, rather than cutting them to grace our kitchen table. It was Henrietta and Bridget from the Land Gardeners who gently teased me about this when they came to visit. They looked around at the gardens at Trematon, overflowing with blooms, and wondered why the house remained bare. They described the ritual of picking flowers – just a few, no more than needed – as like inviting them to a ball. That the flowers want to be chosen, admired, celebrated. That beauty is their purpose, and our appreciation is part of the cycle. These big conversations, that challenged a lot of what I thought I knew, stayed with me long after the plates were cleared.

Regenerative farming was beginning to redefine what true success in farming meant, shifting the focus away from purely quantitative yields towards more qualitative measures such as soil health, biodiversity, nutrition and land resilience, as demonstrated by farms like Riverford. Perhaps most compelling of all, it was also proving that healing didn't have to take generations. If we worked in partnership with Nature's living systems, real regeneration could begin in as little as a year.

And a note on the word regenerative. In recent years, it has entered the mainstream. And while it's galvanising to see the concept gaining ground, with that comes the risk of dilution, of regenerative becoming just another slogan, another layer of greenwash masking the same extractive systems. But for us, within the context of House of Hackney, regeneration is not a promise but a practice and a process. It's a living enquiry, a commitment to leave every part of our business better than how we found it, from the soil to the supply chain, from our people to our products.

Regenerative farming was completely new to us, yet it mirrored so much of the practice we were already undertaking. It gave us both a metaphor and a working model – a glimpse into how Nature's laws and living systems could be entirely transferable to business. As we stood knee-deep in the overgrowth at Trematon, we felt the first murmur of metamorphosis:

What if we applied these same principles of regeneration to business?

It felt as though we were straddling two worlds, trying to midwife a new paradigm of reciprocity and care while still entangled in the old one of extraction. But what was being catalysed in the fields gave us hope. The regenerative agriculture movement was bravely emerging and gaining traction as it met the challenges head on. Against all odds it was offering a proof of concept. And it was showing us, in real time, that another way wasn't just possible – it was already happening.

Could we create a business that restores more than it takes?

Could we set ourselves more holistic measures of success? Not just the yield of profit, but the wellbeing of our people, the integrity of our practices and the regeneration of the natural world around us?

Could our company become as generous, as reciprocal, as life-giving as Nature herself?

What might happen if, instead of forcing growth, we focused on creating the conditions for life to flourish within our organisations, just as regenerative farmers do with the land?

Could there be such a thing as regenerative business practice? Or is that still a paradox waiting to be proven possible?

And inspired by regenerative farming, if more of us began working this way, could it seed a movement strong enough to influence policy, reshape economies and shift the cultural narrative around what business is truly here to do?

————

These were the thoughts swirling in our heads in March 2020 when lockdown hit out of what seemed like nowhere. Suddenly, restrictions were placed around access to Nature. Time outdoors was rationed for the first time in our lives. What had once been abundant and freely available – walks in the woods, jogs in the park, dips in the sea, time spent under open skies – was now strictly bordered by rules and boundaries.

One of the most moving and unexpected outcomes of being collectively grounded was that it sparked what felt like a deep awakening in how we saw the world and our place within it. A kind of shared epiphany about the value we place on Nature. We had been so grossly overlooking the miracle of Nature and our place within it until it was suddenly taken from us, indefinitely. And yet, in that great collective exhale from life as we knew it, a remembering began to flicker and a sense that we were not separate, but part of something vast, intelligent and whole that we are meant to live in tune with. Covid-19 was a steep reminder of the fragility of our ecosystems and the need to protect and maintain that precious equilibrium. That Nature is not a commodity but is, in fact, our community.

For the first time since before the kids were born, I reached for a book. *Small Is Beautiful,* the spine read. The cover was faded, the musty pages tinged with time, but the subtitle stopped me. 'Economics as if People Mattered.' It was by E.F. Schumacher, a name I'd vaguely heard spoken before but didn't know anything about. I'm still not sure where the book came from or how it had ended up in our library, but it seems to have been the book I was meant to read in that moment in time. Little did I know then that it would go on to influence the next chapter of our journey.

Written almost fifty years earlier, it spoke straight to my 2020 thoughts. In a world that had just been brought to a halt, Schumacher's words landed with a radical simplicity. He wrote of the dangers of endless growth, the illusion that 'bigger is better' and the urgent need to return to right relationship – with Nature, with each other, and with meaningful, dignified work. His thinking echoed the spirit of our hero William Morris, who believed that art, labour and beauty all belonged in service of life, not just profit. Both men shared a vision of a more beautiful, human-scale economy rooted in purpose and care.

Small Is Beautiful was a revelation. Long before 'regeneration' became a buzzword, Schumacher was laying the philosophical foundations for a life-honouring economy that challenged the blind pursuit of profit in a finite world and instead asked: what if economics was designed as if people and planet mattered? It felt like a question we were also asking in our own way. Reading *Small Is Beautiful* wasn't the epiphany in how I viewed economics – the seed had already been planted, first through observing Nature's systems, and then through witnessing a real-world example of them in action through regenerative farming. But Schumacher gave that seed shape. He gave me language. And perhaps most importantly, he validated that there was another way to approach economics – one that returned to the original root of the word economy itself: *oikonomia* – the art of household stewardship. As a small company it was empowering to hear that scale isn't a prerequisite for positive change. That small could be beautiful – and deeply impactful.

Just as the second UK lockdown was announced in November 2020, House of Hackney quietly became the first UK interiors brand to be certified B Corp. This marked us, on paper, as part of a growing movement of businesses that value people and planet over profit. B Corp was catalysing a much-needed movement – a collective shift in how business could use its agency for good, bringing these values into the boardroom and encouraging companies to become more aware of their impact to become better stewards of the planet. The 'B' stands for 'benefit' – meaning benefit to all – and being a certified B Corporation means that a business is meeting high standards of social and environmental performance, accountability and transparency, and is legally committed to creating a material positive impact on society and the planet. In practice, it's about balancing the so-called 'triple bottom line' of profit, people and planet. Rather than profit being the only measure of success, the framework insists that a business is equally accountable to its workers, communities and the natural world. The famously rigorous B Corp application, which involved assessing our impact across key areas of governance, workers, community, environment and customers, took us the best part of a year – but in truth, it was a relatively easy process for us. We were already doing the work.

Like many pioneering movements, B Corp has faced growing pains and arguably some questionable decision-making. As it scaled, it began to certify some controversial corporations, most notably Nespresso (Nestlé) in 2022, prompting fierce backlash from within the B Corp community. Critics rightly highlighted Nestle's well-publicised labour issues and environmental impact, with B Corps like Dr. Bronner's publicly questioning the movement's direction. UK brewer BrewDog later lost its certification after reports of a toxic workplace culture, while companies like Scrumbles voluntarily exited, citing a dilution of B Corp's values. Now, however, a correction is underway. In 2025, B Lab, the nonprofit that runs the B Corp network, launched Version 7 of its standards, requiring companies to meet new minimum thresholds across areas like climate action and human rights. Larger businesses face stricter oversight and independent verification. The movement is working to re-anchor itself on the purpose and rigour it expects from the companies who bear its logo, not as a marketing badge, but as a credible tool for systemic change. If it holds itself to the same high standards it asks of others, I know

I'm not alone when I say that B Corp still represents one of the most important, recognised and necessary frameworks for meaningful business impact.

The year-long application process that took place during 2020 coincided with the deep rise in consciousness that Javvy and I were having about the kind of impact we wanted House of Hackney to have. When it arrived, our new B Corp status felt like validation, but it no longer felt like the whole story. It did not yet reflect the higher ambitions we were starting to catch glimpses of: a vision of business not just doing less harm but that was actively restoring life.

We had always operated with a deep sense of responsibility, but year after year, as our awareness expanded, so did our ambitions and the targets we set ourselves for becoming ever more responsible. The more we learned, the more we did.

We were a Living Wage-certified company – a commitment to paying every member of our team not just the minimum wage, but a real living wage, calculated to cover the true cost of living. For us, it was about dignity, fairness and ensuring that the people helping us build this house could thrive, not just get by.

We achieved certified carbon-neutral status, meaning we were measuring, reducing and offsetting our emissions. But we knew neutrality wasn't the end goal. For us, it was just the starting point for regeneration. Even before we were breaking even, we were funnelling sales proceeds into restoration causes. Yes, we needed to be fiscally responsible, but whether we had a profitable year or not we were still using Nature's resources. We felt compelled to name Mother Nature as the inspiration behind our designs and to remunerate Nature almost like a licence to use. Of course, Mother Nature isn't looking to be paid a licence fee, but She does work on the principle of give and take. And it felt important that, in return for using Nature's prints in our designs, we use our sales to restore the ecosystems from which that inspiration was drawn. At House of Hackney, every pattern has a source, and with it comes a responsibility.

So, we began to align ourselves with different charities. For example, after years of seeing leopard print plastered across the high street with no acknowledgement of its source of inspiration – the magnificent big cats or the fragile ecosystems they inhabit – we wanted to pay homage. Profits from our iconic sabre-toothed tiger cushions went directly to the Panthera charity, supporting their work in safeguarding jaguar corridors in Latin America and protecting endangered tiger populations in India.

Our early partnership with Friends of the Earth on our tree-themed wallpaper and textiles evolved into collaborations with the Woodland Trust, where we helped their protection of threatened forests across the UK, and eventually with the World Land Trust. Through them, we now fund the protection of thousands of acres of sacred forest every year: rainforests in Brazil, cloud forests in Ecuador, wildlife corridors in India – living landscapes that are home to endangered species as well as Indigenous communities whose stewardship has always been the truest model of sustainability.

It has always been important to us that every textile we create carries a thread back to the ecosystems we take our inspiration from – through beauty, storytelling, restoration and activism – so that the patterns on our wallpaper or fabric become not just decoration but a reminder of the living worlds we need to honour and protect.

Over time, these micro-partnerships evolved into something bigger – a dedicated 1 per cent of sales restoration fund. Regardless of the kind of year we have, the commitment remains: to honour Nature as a stakeholder.

In fact, I often think about how powerful it would be if this approach became legislation. Imagine if, just as companies pay a licence fee to use a design created by someone else, business was required to pay a small percentage of their sales back to Nature. A simple mechanism to make us pay attention to the source and to ensure that business contributes to restoring what it takes. A licence to Nature – a built-in duty of stewardship, hardwired into the way business operates. The funds could be pooled locally or nationally, or even globally, and distributed through trusted, independent organisations that channel them into protecting biodiversity, restoring the ecosystems and supporting the communities most impacted by ecological breakdown. Just as we already accept corporation tax or VAT, why not a 'Nature Licence Fee'? A visible reminder that no business operates without borrowing from Earth.

Yes, times are tight, but even 1 per cent of sales directed towards protecting Nature would be transformative, and the truth is that we can't afford not to. It would be the best return on investment on anything we could possibly spend our budgets on.

A 1 per cent Nature Licence Fee across UK business as a whole would generate more than **£32 billion every year** for restoring ecosystems, protecting biodiversity and supporting frontline communities.

Of course, some will say that this is simply another tax on business, or that times are too hard to add anything extra. But this is not about placing a burden on business. It is about recognising that business is already borrowing from living systems every single day.

Without Nature, there is no economy. We need fertile soil, clean water, stable climates and thriving communities – this is a licence to continue. The cost of biodiversity collapse and climate breakdown is far greater than the cost of prevention. Regulation is always cheaper than repair.

And yes, critics will call it idealistic, perhaps even unrealistic. But corporate taxation once sounded utopian. So did the NHS. So did maternity leave. So did net-zero commitments. Many of the rights and protections we now take for granted began as 'impossible' ideas.

If reciprocity is the principle, then the other side of the coin is equally important: recognising and rewarding the businesses that actively regenerate the living world. Just as there could be a small fee for using Nature, there could also be tax breaks, reduced business rates or preferential procurement for companies who measurably give back – those who restore biodiversity, build soil health, protect water systems, support Indigenous land guardianship or demonstrate circular, repair-based production models. In other words, rewarding the organisations that actually enhance life, allowing public money to flow to the businesses that replenish the commons rather than those that deplete it. The incentive would be loud and clear: the more companies restore, the more they benefit. Ultimately, this would reframe the very paradigm of business, with success defined not just by what is taken but by what is returned.

In many ways, it echoes the vision of EarthPercent, the movement founded by Brian Eno, to ensure that a share of revenue always flows back to the planet. It began in the music industry with a simple provocation: if you sample or are inspired by the sounds of Nature – birdsong, ocean waves, the rhythm of the rain – shouldn't you give something back to the source? EarthPercent asks musicians, artists and now businesses to pledge a small share of their revenue in recognition of Nature as a silent collaborator in their work, with funds channelled into climate and restoration solutions.

For us, the same principle applies in design. Every House of Hackney print begins with Nature as its muse, whether it's a leopard, a tree or a flower. Just as EarthPercent honours the sounds of Nature in music, we wanted to honour the patterns and forms of Nature in interiors. To acknowledge that these motifs aren't ours to simply extract or commodify, but gifts that carry responsibility. By naming and remunerating Nature, we turn design into reciprocity, beauty in our products translating into protection in the wild. For business, it's just one penny in every pound of sales. But for Nature, it could unlock returns on a scale that shifts the course of our future.

We realised we could no longer be satisfied with the status quo of being 'sustainable', too often interpreted as simply doing less harm when what was needed was urgent renewal and regeneration. The bar had been set too low for too long. Our goal could not be to simply reduce harm – it had to be to restore. What was required was a total paradigm shift, not just in how we did business, but in how we understood our place as participants in the world. We needed to stop seeing business as something separate from Nature, or above it. Because business is part of Nature – and the more we recognise how closely it resembles an ecosystem, the more we realise that to be healthy it must operate by the same rules of interdependence, balance and regeneration.

———

A month later, in December 2020, I turned forty. A milestone made solitary by the circumstance of the pandemic, but in some ways made more profound because of it. Without the possibility of a party, I decided to give myself the very opposite experience – a silent retreat. I'd never even been on a yoga retreat, let alone anything like this. But it felt like the right offering to myself at this crossroads between one version of myself and the woman I was becoming – between the wild uncertainty of youth and the grounded reckoning of middle age. It would be a rare, self-imposed opportunity to truly sit with myself and to try to listen for the quieter voice within. I'll admit I was nervous going in. Afraid of what might rise in the silence. Fearful of boredom, of buried thoughts, of being alone without distraction. But I knew I needed to cross that threshold.

So, I disappeared into the little cabin nestled in the Trematon woods, held in the bosom of the linden trees. No phone. No laptop. Just me, a notebook and a single book, *Anam Ċara* by John O'Donohue, a birthday gift that I grabbed as it arrived in the post that morning. The back cover synopsis sounded like the perfect companion for the moment – something to read and contemplate beside the small fire next to my cast-iron bed. And it was exactly that. The author of *Anam Ċara*, which means 'soul friend' in Irish, was an Irish poet, philosopher and former priest, and the book was a soulful exploration of Celtic wisdom and a reminder of the sacredness of solitude, friendship and inner life. It felt like the perfect companion for the silent soul journey I was about to embark on.

For three days that early December, in between cold-water dips in the estuary, I sat in complete silence. At first, my thoughts were scattered and slow to arrive. I read. I slept. I dreamed deeply. And then, the floodgates opened, and I began to fill the pages of my little red notebook with an outpouring of downloads, my fingers struggling to keep up with the sheer voracity of thoughts. As they bubbled up from my inner sanctum, desperate to be brought to life, these were thoughts and ideas I had never given myself the space to birth.

One strong message came through again and again: a remembering of the flourishing of life. I found myself staring at the fireside wooden chair, the patchwork quilt that kept me warm at night and the little copper mirror over the washstand, and thought about their journeys of becoming. What was the story of the fibres? Had they been grown with care or poisoned with pesticides? Had the trees been harvested mindfully or plundered from exhausted land? Was the chair carved by happy hands in dignified work or by someone undervalued and underpaid? And the mirror – was its copper drawn from the earth responsibly or at the expense of soil health, water systems and the communities nearby?

Sitting with myself activated my awakening to truly thinking about the full journey of a product, from the life of the fibres to the felling of the tree. We had always cared deeply about the factories who made our product and the relationships we had with them. But now my thinking was deepening to the very roots of the journey of supply. I began to wonder about every stage, every hand, every ecosystem touched along the way. This curiosity would eventually crystallise into a vision of an end-to-end regenerative cycle in which every stage and element of making a product was considered. Back then, I didn't yet have the language for it. But the seed had been planted, and it was beginning to take root.

That time in the cabin marked the beginning of a new decade. I was hungry for meaningful change. It felt as if I was crossing the threshold from the Mother to the Wise Woman archetype. The Mother creates and holds; the Wise Woman sees and teaches. She no longer seeks approval, she embodies truth, is the gatekeeper of memory and lives in deep service to what matters most. I knew it was time to step into my stage, my age of responsibility and honour the wisdom that was beginning to take root.

My co-pilot, Javvy, and I were ready to lead House of Hackney on a journey towards regeneration; a journey with possibly no destination that we would be lifelong students of. Not just in what we were creating, but in how we lived, how we worked, and how we contributed to the world around us. But to do so we needed to learn about how to become regenerative in a business context.

CHAPTER 11

Chrysalis

'The heart that breaks open can contain the whole universe.'
Joanna Macy, *World as Lover, World as Self*

The more I normalised working outside, the more I began to track the seasons, welcoming the signs of life returning with the annual rebirth of the earth, even when the signs were not yet visible. I swear I could feel the rising underground energy stirring not long after the winter solstice had passed. As I became more attuned to the seasons, I began to notice a sharp drop in my own energy around Halloween, at the same time as the light dipped. At first, I put it down to hormonal changes, but year after year I started to track the same seasonal plummet. And yet I'd keep pushing through at the same pace I had at the zenith of the year, demanding a summer energy from a winter body. I was overriding my natural rhythms, ignoring what Nature so clearly demonstrates – that we wax and wane in rhythm with the seasons.

In the January of the second winter lockdown, with nowhere to rush to and the headlines bleak, for the first time, I allowed myself to hibernate, just as Nature intended. I noticed how deeply my family slept, how we naturally woke with the sun, instead of the jolt of an alarm in the pitch-black morning. At first, it felt quite indulgent, but the usual jet-lagged fog that haunted dark winter mornings started to lift. Our kids were more settled too. Without the stress of dragging them out of bed in the cold and dark, and with the extra sleep they needed as growing children in a time of wintering, the usual morning resistance softened. The sibling bickering even lessened when their bodies were charged to optimum and their systems more soothed and energised.

This unexpected experiment opened my eyes to our primal need to live in tune with our circadian rhythms: the internal clocks that are biologically hardwired to guide our bodies through a twenty-four-hour cycle that governs our sleep, mood and metabolism. Influenced by the light and the dark, they affect our bodies as the seasonal light energises us in the summer and roots us in the winter, as it works in tune with the waxing and waning of the seasonal shifts.

That winter, without alarm clocks, I was able to realise how deeply my energy, focus and mood were affected by the light around me and how much better we could all feel when we surrendered to its rhythm. How much of our struggle in winter isn't just the cold or the dark, but the resistance to the season itself.

We are children of the sun. No matter how advanced our tech becomes, we can't override the biological truth that our internal systems rise and set with the light. When we honour these rhythms, our bodies function at their best. But the constructs and expectations of modern life often pull us in the opposite direction. We wake before sunrise to the shrill of alarms, we spend most of our day indoors under artificial lighting, often under the glow of screens until late into the night. This disconnection from our natural rhythms and habitat is resulting in a sense of chronic disruption to our own bodies.

Waking with the sun felt so intuitively right. Having time in the workday to connect with Nature, to track the seasons, wasn't just restorative, it was wholly transformative. Everyone deserves this feeling of life force as a natural state. I began to wonder, what would it look like if we structured life around our natural rhythms and habitats and become more aligned with the systems and environment our bodies and spirits are built to engage with?

On the surface it might sound radical, but reclaiming this state of aliveness is the most natural action we could take. Truly honouring our bodies and the cycles of the living world isn't new, it's ancient. It's in our nature.

It was our first big step towards reimagining that relic, the forty-hour week, a system born in the Industrial Revolution, turning one hundred in 2026. Outdated now and never designed with real wellbeing in mind. We recognised that a brilliant team, supported by efficient systems, deserves to be rewarded with the gift of time. Time that should have been returned to us with every leap in productivity, but which capitalism never sanctioned.

What if we returned to our birthright, our place within Nature, not just on weekends or retreats, but as part of everyday life? In our working weeks, in our schools, in our homes?

What if our workplaces, schools and institutions were designed to support our innate nature – acknowledging light, rest, movement and seasonal rhythms as essential to human thriving?

What if time in Nature was a daily norm, woven into our workdays and school days, not as an afterthought or treat but as a core part of how we live?

How I wanted this for our children.

How I wanted this for our team.

We had already been early adopters of the four-day week, running it seasonally from April to August since 2019, echoing the quieter rhythm of our workload and the peak energy of the year. It enabled the team to enjoy five months of light-filled days of long weekends in Nature.

So, we introduced the concept of 'winter hours' for the remainder of the year – from September to March – with a 4pm finish time to honour the body's call for more rest, quiet and recalibration at this time of the year. Even though this was our busiest half, with the highest sales targets, a shorter working day didn't feel like a risk to the business. Nature had become a compass we trusted deeply to guide us. Mimicking Her rhythms felt not only intuitive, but wise. Fewer hours with a healthy, embodied team made far more business sense than pushing through with an overworked, disconnected one.

And in the process, unknowingly we were entering into a more reciprocal relationship with our team. As in Nature, where reciprocity is a sacred law, what we care for nurtures us in return. We saw that when we gave our team space to harmonise their with natural seasonal rhythms, they gave back with energy, creativity and commitment. Reciprocity is relational not transactional and, when we honoured that principle, the business flourished alongside its people.

———

When in January 2021 the third lockdown was announced, my first reaction, like everyone's, was despondency and frustration at yet another round of confinement and uncertainty. Once I'd moved past that, I decided to settle in and see this pause as a rare window of time where I wasn't split between Cornwall and London. With Nature still in retreat and life in wintering mode, it felt like a chance to bed in, bundle up on the sofa and immerse myself in learning what becoming regenerative in business might actually mean. I approached the study of regeneration the same way I would any subject I was trying to self-teach – by googling, ordering and devouring every book I could find on the topic.

One breadcrumb led to the next as I tumbled down rabbit holes, tracing citations, references and footnotes, each one bringing with it a new haul of books from the postman, becoming almost forensic in my quest to understand it. I felt I had to fully grasp the principles if I was to hope to embed something as potentially paradigm-shifting as regeneration into our company.

It was a revelation to discover that the model of regeneration existed beyond farming, and there was such a thing as the field of regenerative economics – an approach that sees the economy not as a machine to be optimised, but as a living system that thrives through balance, mutual exchange and renewal. At the time, there was far more written about regenerative economics than regenerative business itself, but, ultimately, an economy is simply the sum of its businesses. I figured that if I could understand these foundational principles, I might begin to explore how we could apply them to a living, breathing company like ours.

What I found was a trove of thinking – foundational works like *The Limits to Growth*, the seminal 1972 study co-authored by Donella Meadows, which warned of the ecological and economic consequences of unchecked growth and introduced the sobering truth: 'Unlimited growth on a finite planet is impossible.'

I followed it with *Doughnut Economics* by Kate Raworth, which proposed a pioneering but pragmatic economic framework for meeting the human needs in an economy while respecting the planetary boundaries. From there, Giles Hutchins' work on systems leadership and business inspired by Nature's patterns, first articulated in his 2012 book *The Nature of Business*, demonstrated how organisations can flourish by aligning with the same principles that allow natural systems to thrive. Giles's work led me to *Designing Regenerative Cultures* by Daniel Wahl, which quickly became a dog-eared bible as we began actively embedding the concept of regeneration into our company and culture.

Alongside the theory-heavy texts, I was equally moved by more lyrical works. There were big new stories being unearthed at that time. Many were ancient truths bubbling back to the surface, finding fertile ground in that moment of death followed by emergence. These were narratives with the power to shift the cultural lens. The power of storytelling was offering not just information, but keys to the transformation we were collectively searching for. They were worlds that could be re-found, if we fostered them. Books like Robin Wall Kimmerer's *Braiding Sweetgrass* and *The Mother Tree* by Suzanne Simard both blew my mind and opened my eyes to the sentience and intelligence of the living world in their poetic, unforgettable ways.

I remember the first wild strawberries appearing that June and, since having read Kimmerer's words, seeing them differently – as tiny, beating hearts of the earth inviting us to remember our place in the great web of life. Around this time, I started to notice the thirst for Indigenous wisdom rising fast in our Western cultures, led by voices like Kimmerer, Winona LaDuke and Vandana Shiva. They offered new but ancient worldviews grounded not in domination, but in relationship and reverence, reminding us that another way was possible – if we chose to remember it. And what made this more powerful was that Indigenous people had proven themselves to be the most effective stewards of the natural world against all odds, despite centuries of colonisation, land theft and cultural erasure.

What fascinated me, too, was the long-term stewardship embedded in so many Indigenous cultures. It was so radically different from the Western mindset of short-term extraction for maximum profit, without consideration for future generations, ecological balance or our collective wellbeing. In Indigenous cosmologies, care for the land is inseparable from care for community, and the future is honoured as deeply as the past. For example, the Haudenosaunee principle of considering the impact of decision-making on the next seven generations was some of the most profound systems thinking I'd ever encountered (thinking that we would later start to implement at House of Hackney). These weren't just spiritual beliefs; they were holistic frameworks for governance, ecology and leadership. Without the tools or frameworks of modern economics, they had proven themselves to be the world's greatest stewards because they never saw the land as something to own, extract from or conquer, but as a relative to be respected, a relationship to be nurtured. They offered models of decentralised decision-making, collective responsibility and ecological interdependence rooted in Nature's own blueprint – everything I was beginning to seek as a business leader navigating a broken system. It felt as though the wisdom of the past was starting to surface as a map to emerging worlds.

And in lands closer to where I was, Celtic writers were surfacing similar truths. They reminded us of an older way of seeing, rooted in the pagan understanding that the land is animate, conscious and sacred. Sharon Blackie's *If Women Rose Rooted* shone a powerful remembering on a time when humans lived in deep relationship with Earth and the natural world was revered as kin, not commodified as resource. Diana Beresford-Kroeger's *To Speak for the Trees* spoke with that same reverence through both a scientific and a spiritual lens. Drawing from Celtic wisdom, plant biology and ecological storytelling, she reminded me of the ancient Brehon law contracts between people and forests – agreements of reciprocity, protection and respect. My ancestors knew the importance of being in the right relationship with the land.

And perhaps they still hold the map back to that belonging. That's what I was trying to do – to listen to the myriad voices of elders, philosophers, economists, writers and, of course, the garden itself. They all brought the same message that everything is connected. That we belong to a larger whole. That the systems we build must mimic the living systems of Earth – diverse, circular, adaptive and deeply relational. That Nature isn't a resource, but a teacher, a mother, a healer, a systems thinker. Business, if designed with care, can become a form of stewardship. These books brought with them an invitation to design differently – organisations, systems, products, education, life – and that the purpose of our companies is to design for the flourishing of life.

———

In a time when it felt like the old paradigms of politics, economics and even identity were collapsing in front of our eyes, and governments were proving themselves increasingly untrustworthy, their lockdown hypocrisies and backroom deals revealing a rot at the core, we turned our attention elsewhere. To ancient wisdom anchored in Nature: in reciprocity, reverence and right relationship with the living world. In plants we could trust.

It wasn't long before my research led me to the website of a place called Schumacher College, named after E.F. Schumacher, whose book *Small Is Beautiful* had crystallised my vision of creating a business that truly valued people and planet. The college was founded on principles drawn directly from that philosophy. Nestled in the South Devon countryside in a building called The Old Postern, set in the grand medieval estate of Dartington Hall, it looked as though it had been lifted straight from a storybook. Schumacher College was a truly magical place and not just aesthetically but in how it taught its students holistically, ecologically and spiritually. It stood as a beacon for a different kind of learning that wove together a head, heart and hands approach into an embodied way of being as it taught its students not just ideas but also cultivated true transformation.

I was amazed to discover that this hotbed of everything I was gravitating towards was located just over the border in Devon, barely a half an hour drive from Trematon. The ethos of Schumacher College was greatly inspired by the Deep Ecology movement, a philosophical and activist tradition developed by thinkers like Arne Naess and Joanna Macy that called for a radical shift in how we perceive our place in the great web of life. At its foundation was a challenging of the anthropocentric worldview – the assumption that human beings sit at the centre of existence – and instead it promoted the idea that every species, every organism, has intrinsic value, not just human life. Through the college,

I encountered thinkers who would go on to profoundly shape my ideas and the path we were beginning to forge: people like Satish Kumar, whose books *Soil, Soul, Society* and *Radical Love* left a deep imprint on me about how to lead business with love and humility; Stephan Harding, whose teachings on Gaia theory helped me see Earth as a living, breathing, self-regulating organism; and James Lovelock, the visionary scientist behind the Gaia hypothesis, who gave scientific language to what Indigenous and ancestral wisdom had long known: that Mother Earth is alive, intelligent and deeply interconnected with all life on Earth.

So, when Schumacher College announced a new course – An Introduction to Regenerative Business – I signed up immediately. It was the first course to run after the college reopened after the lockdown. The course had been put together by Jenny Mackewn – an elder in the field of transformational leadership. With no formal background in business, she was free from the shackles of conventional business thinking and brought intuitive wisdom and an extraordinary line-up of guest speakers and facilitators. We were introduced to the concept of doughnut economics by Erinch Sahan, who helped us see how business could sit within planetary boundaries while serving human thriving.

At Riverford Farm, Guy Singh-Watson generously walked us through their journey towards truly regenerative farming and employee ownership. Later, we sat in circle with Kim and Paul Polman. (Kim is the co-founder of Reboot the Future, and Paul is the former Unilever CEO who pioneered a journey towards corporate sustainability and was now championing regeneration as author of Net Positive.) The message was clear and urgent: even global corporations could be reimagined as forces for regeneration. They offered their hard-won wisdom openly to us, holding nothing back, committed to lighting the way for the next generation of regenerative business leaders.

While all of this fed the head, our hearts were also tenderly tended to. Sitting under the canopy of redwoods, Satish Kumar, co-founder of Schumacher College, then in his eighty-fifth year yet carrying the verve of a young man, spoke softly and simply of a beautiful model of economics grounded not in extraction but in love, ecology and care. With a glint in his eye, he regaled us with a story of giving a lecture at the London School of Economics, where he challenged the students: 'You call yourselves the London School of Economics, but this isn't real economics. Its roots – *oikos*, home, and *nomia*, stewardship – are about caring for our shared home. So, tell me: where is the teaching on how to care for the only home we have – our planet?'

During a rare sun-drenched February lunch outside Schumacher's canteen, an impeccably dressed gentleman pedalled up on his bike to our table and braked with a smile. From a shoulder bag, he drew a Venezuelan cuatro, a small, four-string guitar. 'Mind if I join you?' he asked, pulling up a chair as if we'd been expecting him all along. This was my first encounter with Stephan Harding, co-founder of Schumacher College and a writer known for his work on holistic science and the Gaia hypothesis. He urged us to stretch our imaginations far beyond the present moment and took us on a deep-time walk, into the vast intelligence of Earth herself, where our human era is no more than a blink. The week was turning out to be the most extraordinary kind of educational experience, not in a classroom but in a field, in a forest, under a night sky and over shared meals. Stephan would sadly pass just two years later, in September 2024. In poignant symmetry, it was the very same month that Schumacher College was forced to close its doors.

I returned for its final course, not as a student this time, but as a speaker, invited to present the regenerative journey of House of Hackney as a case study. It should have felt like a full-circle moment. But as I took my place in the presentation chair, in the centre of the circle where I had once listened wide-eyed, the tears slowly rolled. Fighting them, I remembered that I was there to inspire this last cohort with another way. To give back what had been given to me. To honour the transformational leaders and wisdom keepers who had inspired me. Now, with its closure, where were we to go to find that kind of wisdom and nourishment? But there is some hope. Whispers of a search for a new space that might rise from the ashes; and perhaps bring with it new life and new ideas, and sometimes I wonder… Maybe that's the higher purpose of Trematon. A place where the kind of seeds planted at Schumacher can continue to grow. Maybe, once the children have grown and life shifts, Trematon's next chapter is to become a living school, where we learn to weave ecology, imagination and regenerative action into daily life.

But the challenge now was leaving this incubator of big vision and taking it into the real world with me. It became a year of study – like a master's degree by moonlight. I had a tower of books on my bedside table, often several on the go at once. One foot still in the conventional model, the other slowly sinking into something older and deeper.

Looking back, this was our chrysalis phase: a tender, liminal stage of dissolution and reformation where nothing seemed outwardly to be happening. No one would have noticed much, but deep down, everything was shifting. I say 'our' because, while I was reading the books, Javvy was doing the work too. But his classroom was the garden. While I pored over the texts, he was outside listening and observing deeply; consciously connecting to the land and tracking how quickly it was healing. How the biodiversity was returning. Like the caterpillar that dissolves into some formless goo before it becomes a butterfly, we were in a process of unlearning, absorbing, reconfiguring. And a caterpillar gives no sign that its higher emergence is a butterfly.

What we were now seeing, we couldn't unsee. Everything had changed. And to stay true to ourselves and to our purpose, we couldn't ignore it. We had to try to embed the principles we were learning.

How were we going to introduce this to our team – and establish it – so that we could activate them to join us on an even deeper journey of learning and unlearning all we thought we knew about being a company? An unknown path, a path we needed to scythe into existence ourselves. One that would challenge almost everything we'd been taught to believe about business and organisation. But at the same time, it echoed everything we were learning from Nature's living systems.

The core vision was simple: to design a company that honours life.

In its products. In its operations. In its governance, accounting, culture and community.

To follow life's principles: of regeneration, interdependence, reciprocity, diversity, adaptability.

Because every other living system thrives under these principles.

So surely it could work for us too?

CHAPTER 12

Metamorphosis

'You never change things by fighting the existing reality. To change something, build a new model that makes the existing model obsolete.'

Paraphrased from Buckminster Fuller, *Think Out of the Box*

Like a true ecosystem where each species plays an integral part in its success, we understood that if we were serious about beginning the journey towards becoming a regenerative business, we'd need the participation and creativity of our team and our suppliers. The mission would need to go well beyond mine and Javvy's vision.

We knew our first step was to introduce Sam, who by now had been promoted to managing director, to what we were thinking. At the time, I remember wishing that we had a case study to show her, a success story of a company that was further along the way and was *proof* that a business rooted in the principles of living systems and integrated in Nature made good business sense! All we had was the proof that it had been certainly successful for Nature for billions of years and, as we were but a company of biological beings, based on this hypothesis, we should take our cue from Nature's business plan – a 3.7-billion-year blueprint for resilience. In its pages lay the only model of true resilience proven to thrive in the face of change.

What we were proposing was a wholesale rethink of how we do business, a total paradigm shift and redesign of its purpose. I knew it was going to take a lot of work to do it deeply in a company that already felt as though it was at its maximum capacity. It would also mean that, as we moved from a position of extraction to restoration, it was likely that we would have to cut off supply chains and revenue streams that no longer aligned with the regenerative mission. It did feel like a big risk and Sam, a fierce protector of the company and its people, raised some questions with her analytical and cautious mind – and a sobering dose of heavy pragmatism.

Sam liked the vision, but there were so many unknowns and potential risks. Could we really do it without potentially risking the stability of the company? Could we afford the investment? Could we afford to roll back on the sales of the products and materials that would no longer stand up to the scrutiny needed for a mission like this? Did we have the time and the bandwidth to do this when workloads already felt stretched? We listened carefully to her – Sam's opinions were very valid and there were many unknowns. Ultimately, the aim was the opposite of destabilising the business – this was about using the principles of Nature to strengthen the company, making it more resilient and creating more health and abundance for its ecosystem participants.

Although it was uncharted territory for us, deep down, Javvy and I knew the risk of standing still was greater than the risk of moving forwards. Sam, with her sharp mind balanced by a deep intuitive intelligence, knew in her heart the same truth. And we had strong trust and respect for each other. Though she voiced her concerns – as any good managing director should – she understood that this was not just a business strategy; it was a necessity for our future.

We had recently hired Kellie, a super-seasoned sustainability consultant with a view to improving our product journey (which, at surface level, wasn't terrible due to our size and mostly made-to-order model, but there were many unknown areas we needed to understand). We soon brought Kellie into the conversation around regeneration. Like the rest of us, she was new to it, but we could see immediately that she shared our palpable excitement to really move the dial. Kellie had been an early pioneer in the sustainability space, having helped brands like Burberry and Vivienne Westwood migrate to less extractive supply chains, but even she was beginning to feel the limits, and the frustration, of 'sustaining' a status quo that was already failing.

Together, across twelve weeks, we enrolled in a course on regenerative business led by John Fullerton at the Capital Institute, who introduced us to the 'eight principles of regenerative economics'. John brought rigour and realism to how they could be introduced in a business context. He showed they weren't just abstract ideals, but patterns drawn from how living systems thrive. The principles gave us the start of a language to begin imagining how House of Hackney might evolve to become a measurably regenerative business, not just sustaining our business touchpoints but actively leaving them better than how we found them. Nature is inherently regenerative, and its principles act as a blueprint for creating an economy whose businesses promote shared abundance and ecological and social wellbeing, creating a more equitable future for all life on Earth.

The eight principles we learned and our approach to them are as follows.

1. In Right Relationship

We learned that the human economy doesn't hover above Earth, it's embedded within it and utterly dependent on it. Everything is connected, and damage in one place ripples everywhere else. For us, this reframed the business entirely: we were not separate from Nature but a participant inside Her systems. At the time, we didn't yet know how to turn this into a practical step, but this thinking would eventually lead us to appoint Mother Nature and Future Generations to our board, literally giving Her a voice in every decision.

2. Views Wealth Holistically

Wealth is more than money in the bank. It's the wellbeing of the whole – people, planet, culture and spirit – flourishing together. This would become the lens for looking beyond profit to the health of our entire ecosystem: supply chains, communities, ecosystems and creativity. At the time, our metrics were almost entirely financial, and this principle made us realise how partial our definition of success had been. Later, our IP&L (integrated profit and loss) work would make this tangible, revealing the value we create in human, natural, social and produced capital, not just financial capital.

3. Innovative, Adaptive, Responsive

Darwin never meant 'survival of the strongest' but survival of those who are best matched to their environment. We started to realise that becoming more adaptable and agile was going to be essential to our future resilience. This new mindset helped us shift from 'sustainable' to 'regenerative' thinking and we began to redesign our products and processes to align with the living systems that sustain us.

4. Empowered Participation

In a true living system, every part has a fundamental role to play. Health comes when each element not only meets its own needs but contributes its gifts to the whole. We would later see this in practice when we moved from top-down departmental plans to co-created regenerative roadmaps, where each team designed their own approach, rooted in their skills and creativity, and the mission came alive. At the time, we were probably still holding the reins too tightly – this principle would challenge us to loosen our grip and allow for more co-creation and participation.

5. Honours Community and Place

Every community has its own flavour and pulse shaped by its land, its history and people. We realised that our work needed to move away from the usual homogenised model of capitalism, and reflect and support the localities we touched, from our home in Hackney to our fabric mills in the north of England and the regenerative cotton farms we were starting to work with in India. That meant championing local strengths, celebrating their unique culture and ensuring employment was meaningful and participatory for the community rather than imposing a one-size-fits-all approach.

6. Edge Effect Abundance

Nature shows us that edges – where two different systems meet – are teeming with life. We started to think about how to foster those kinds of fertile edges in our own work: cross-department collaboration, supplier input, even customer participation in shaping our regenerative journey.

7. Robust Circulatory Flow

Just as blood keeps a body alive, healthy economies need circulation – of money, materials, ideas and resources – so that no part is starved. We saw the importance of ensuring value flowed fairly through our system, from suppliers to customers. Until then, we'd been mostly about the circulation of money – our 1 per cent of sales for restoration work was one way to keep resources cycling back into the living world – but this principle widened our view to every form of value: the flow of natural value (like clean air, fertile soil and biodiversity), human value (skills, creativity and wellbeing), social value (trust, equity and community resilience) and cultural value (stories, traditions and meaning). When these circulate well, the whole system thrives.

8. Seeks Balance

A living system isn't static but a constant, living adjustment towards equilibrium. Regenerative systems deftly balance the need for resilience and efficiency, collaboration and competition, diversity and unity. For us, this meant resisting the pressure for constant growth at all costs and instead finding a rhythm that balanced the needs of our people community, our supply and factory community and our Nature community in equal measure. At the time, this felt like the most radical principle of all – because it meant a total paradigm shift, redefining 'success' itself.

———

It was really useful that we could do the course together in real time and afterwards work through each principle and workshop with a view to how these principles might be applied to House of Hackney. But there was a lot of head scratching as it was still largely quite academic and philosophical, and there were few examples of the principles embedded in real companies. There seemed to be so many thinkers in the space – brilliant, visionary, expansive brains – but not necessarily doers. No one that I came across was working inside a company, let alone running one, and understood the limitations, trade-offs and expectations that came with it. None of them had actually migrated a business towards being a regenerative business. I appreciated and was inspired by the big thinking. I was a big thinker too. But where were the practical applications? Where were the case studies? The learnings? The metrics, even, to begin with? Had any companies truly pushed this work into the real world?

Later, I would discover Interface, who were pioneers of industrial sustainability through closed-loop systems and carbon-negative carpets. They were a company that had spent decades proving that business could not just reduce its footprint but could actually reverse it. Along the way I would also come across Vivo Barefoot, whose founders were redefining the relationship between business, body and biome, and were making footwear designed to restore natural movement and support planetary health in the process. Further afield in LA, the womenswear brand Christy Dawn was growing regenerative cotton in partnership with Indian farmers and even inviting customers to co-invest in the protection of the farms. And in the UK, Elvis & Kresse were turning what were waste streams to anyone else, stuff like decommissioned fire hoses, into beautifully crafted, circular luxury handbags and donating 50 per cent of their profits to social causes, with a commitment to regeneration by 2030. These were businesses who were not just talking about change but actively integrating regeneration into their work, each in their own unique way weaving Nature into product design, supply chains and purpose.

And yet, even as these companies honoured pieces of the regenerative puzzle, there didn't seem to be a full blueprint for what we were beginning to imagine: a company where Nature was integrated not just in products but across every level – governance, organisation, finance, community. There was no clear model out there that fully embodied the worldview we were starting to glimpse or offered a practical map for others to follow.

Going it alone was going to be a challenge, but it didn't deter us. By then, we were fully signed up as a management team to the idea of becoming regenerative. We made Kellie our head of regeneration, to honour her role as our guide on the path. Of course, we were all students on this journey and to figure out what regeneration could look like for House of Hackney, we had to embrace our intuition – to feel our way through, not just think our way through. Luckily, we had a lot of that. From my year of deep research, I was struck by how many of the voices leading this big, systemic thinking were women: Rachel Carson, Joanna Macy, Janine Benyus, Kate Raworth, Robin Wall Kimmerer, Rebecca Solnit, Vandana Shiva, Naomi Klein, Donella Meadows and so many more. They were not just theorists, but visionaries, bridge-builders and truth-tellers. I began to notice that there was something about the feminine, about the embodied, relational, life-giving nature of womanhood, that lent itself to this work of imagining more connected, life-affirming systems. An innate sense of care, of stewardship, of interdependence. Or maybe a deeper willingness to listen – to the earth, to intuition, to each other – and to hold complexity without rushing to control it.

So, we put our heads together.

Two things were clear. Firstly, we needed to define what a regenerative journey looked like for House of Hackney so that the whole team could get behind it. Secondly, we knew that the mission, like Nature herself, would need the active participation of everyone in our business ecosystem, who each had a fundamental role to play in it. We wanted people to be able to bring their purpose to work every day. To know that their work was not just a job, but a chance to contribute their gifts to something larger than themselves, something alive and meaningful.

We already had some solid foundations.

As majority shareholders, as long as we didn't rock the health of the company, we had the freedom to take the path we felt called to. And now, with the support of our senior team, we were ready to get going. When it came time to present our vision to the wider team, it helped that Sam and Kellie were such grounded, inspiring leaders – it no longer felt like a founder's wild idea, but more of a necessary, collective commitment to honouring our brand muse, Mother Nature.

With a team of about fifty people based across our London and New York offices, we were the perfect size for the incubation of new ideas and ways of doing. Small enough to be agile, to take risks and foster collaboration; big enough to test and learn in meaningful ways, and to hold real agency with suppliers who we needed on this journey with us.

The culture at House of Hackney was already pretty collaborative, feminine-leaning and intuitive, and it really helped that as we began to move towards becoming regenerative, there was an absence of any big ego. This culture of selflessness mattered because regeneration is not about extraction or awards for the few, but about the health and flourishing of the whole.

We live in a wider culture that celebrates the left brain – reductionist, logical and analytical – and we have an economy that rewards the same. If we are to shift towards a regenerative way of working, we need to reclaim the gifts of the right brain: intuitive, creative, collaborative, empathetic, storytelling, systems-seeing, caring. This reorientation, this paradigm shift, is not just part of the work but at the heart of it. We were lucky: we already had a lot of right-brain intelligence in the company; and now it was time to consciously harness it.

And it felt like a fresh start. The paint was drying on our beautiful new House of Hackney headquarters of St Michael's – a former Victorian clergy house and adjoining schoolhouse set in a hidden enclave of ecclesiastical buildings in Shoreditch, built around a little community square. A more perfect London home we couldn't imagine. Although we were now off the beaten track and away from the high street, we were happy to be back in the type of liminal peripheral space where we felt most at ease, where the seekers could find us if they looked hard enough. Our new home opened onto a rare pocket of green – St Mark's Square – a small oasis in the middle of the city and a place time seemed to have forgotten as the City's Gotham-like skyline rose up around it. Everyone was excited about the move, and it felt like a bright new chapter in our story. And with that feeling of renewal, it seemed the right moment to bring the whole team together for our first all-team meeting in our new home of St. Michael's and introduce the journey we were about to embark on.

I was nervous about what was at stake – and the stakes were high. We needed the team to grasp something far beyond what we've been indoctrinated to think about business. We needed them to be moved by the mission, to feel inspired enough to play an active role in bringing it to life. And we needed everyone.

We decided the best way forwards was to appeal to them personally – to show how this shift could make their own lives healthier, more abundant, more fulfilling. The premise was that if we take care of the conditions that sustain life, the natural outcomes will be health, resilience and abundance for everyone.

I started by taking them through a future vision of a company – what a day in the life of House of Hackney in 2030 could look like. It was largely modelled on what I'd experienced at Schumacher (soon after, we would send our team there to experience it for themselves) and it showed a company that was embodied in head, heart and hands – everything we wanted to become. But I realised later that it probably sounded too wild, too beautiful to be a business, too far removed from what we've been conditioned to believe a company should be.

Sam and Kellie set the scene around the climate emergency we were facing (with the UK becoming the first country to declare one in May 2019), and how we believed in the opportunity for SMEs – ours included – to use our entrepreneurial spirit and agency to pioneer a new model of business. One that restored more than it took, if we followed Nature's lead in how She organises herself. That this was the driving force behind our shift, alongside our desire to cultivate a deeper sense of holistic health for our company, for the people and communities we touched and for the planet itself. A model where there would be upsides and benefits for everyone. We then shared our new mission statement to reflect this vision. But in our enthusiasm, we crucially forgot that a living ecosystem is always a co-creation. Instead of inviting the team into the creation process, we presented them with a ready-made plan for each department, totally missing the opportunity to shape it together.

It was April, the time of our financial year-end, and we'd had a good year. Those pandemic years had ended up being strong sales years for the interiors sector as people focused on making their homes more beautiful. We closed the gathering by putting our money where our mouth was. To show that this was truly a collective effort, we decided that instead of bonuses rewarding only managers, we would split the profit equally across everyone at every level in the company. This was no longer shareholder primacy – it was an all-company stakeholding. The gesture went down very well and we felt a wave of relief, sensing we'd landed our new mission.

When the clapping died down, Kellie took the floor and spoke about the need for us to use our team talents of creativity, influence and activism to help shift the cultural narrative – in the spirit of William Morris, whose aesthetic and ethos infused our work. She asked everyone to come together as a company at the upcoming Climate March happening in just a couple of weeks.

The march was on a Friday, which was normally our day off under the four-day week, so it meant people choosing to come in for it. We wanted to make activism participatory, fun and creative, so together we made beautiful banners with the artist Rob Ryan and then gathered to march as part of the Business Declares collective. Only a quarter of the team showed up, and apart from Aesop, we seemed to be the only other brand there. It was quite disappointing. At first it made us question whether we had a team as serious as we were about Nature integration and protection. But then we began to question our own approach.

There were a few now glaringly obvious things we'd missed. We got a few things right and others less so… But, really, there are no true mistakes, just learnings, because it was all part of the process, part of the enquiry, as we tried to intuit our way through it.

So, we went back to the drawing board. We created a framework: a series of questions designed to prompt ideas from them, to help each department build out their own map, drawing on their unique gifts and talents as a team. We invited them to go into Nature together and ideate both for their own departments and for the wider business. When people came back into the room after the exercise, something had shifted, they were ignited, a fire in their bellies stoked. They came up with stronger ideas, deeper insights and fresh lines of enquiry, which everyone shared passionately – even the quieter voices.

One assumption had been that our team already had a strong connection to Nature, but many were young, urban-based and without regular access to green spaces. My own bond with the natural world had only deepened when we'd been given a garden to care for, so why had I imagined theirs would be fully formed?

Like Nature, we learned that we couldn't expect immediate change – we had to unlearn that mindset. It takes nourishing the root with the right conditions over time; the changes are not always visible to the naked eye before the shoots come through. And contrary to the typical business focus on outcomes, this was about focusing on the process – and letting the outcomes emerge. (Something we haven't always managed – we, too, still sometimes slip into key performance indicators and outcomes as measures of progress or proof for the wider business community, who are not always comfortable with what we can't track.)

Another gap was education. Regeneration, with all its principles and layers of meaning, isn't something that clicks instantly. It requires unlearning as much as learning, and even after my year of deep study I was still trying to wrap my head around it. Expecting others to grasp it without that foundation was unrealistic, even if I had come to believe it was something already alive in each of us. So, we put a big emphasis on education – from inviting urban growers, grassroots charities and activists to engage the team on their missions to fostering internal knowledge – sharing through our company monthly 'regen sessions'. Perhaps most importantly, we ensured the team had enough time in the field during work hours – to learn directly from the greatest teacher of them all: Nature.

We started to understand that people protect what they love, and they love what they feel connected to. And that connection needed to be nurtured inside the work environment – which we would incorporate into a Time With Nature policy, setting up and encouraging people to spend time connecting to Nature in the working week.

A business that honoured Nature naturally felt like a paradox to some of the team. There were doubters, asking why be in business if we're contributing harm at all? But that misses the deeper point. No human activity is impact-free; the real question is whether our footprint is destructive or regenerative. Businesses – especially SMEs – hold a unique opportunity to shift culture, supply chains and ways of working. It's not about opting out; it's about showing up differently. Like breathing, participation is unavoidable – the challenge is to become conscious participants, giving back more than we take and using our agency to become a net contributor to life. Opting out changes little. But reimagining from within just might change everything. Change is difficult. People are often shy to change, even in a small, agile company of people who inherently want to do the right thing. It calls for patience, humility, transparency, co-creation and close communication – qualities we realised we needed to deepen.

This co-creation became our regenerative roadmap – a living guide shaped, co-authored by everyone. From that point, we no longer saw our team as just employees, but as ambassadors of this movement – people who, in their day-to-day lives, could use their influence to share regenerative ways with their own touchpoints: customers, housemates, families.

We've noticed natural peaks and troughs in motivation around the mission. At times, a solution can feel so far out of reach, so beyond our influence entirely, then suddenly something unlocks, and the path becomes clear. One such moment was the development of our regenerative cotton velvet in 2025. Just a year earlier, even our long-time supplier, British Velvet, had felt it was impossible – the industry simply wasn't set up to work regeneratively. But the company's founder, now a grandparent, began to see the future through the eyes of his grandchildren, and that vision became the catalyst for change. Together, we coaxed the idea into being, creating the first truly regenerative British velvet. And, in turn, supporting farming systems that restore soil health, increase biodiversity, capture carbon and bring vitality back to ecosystems long degraded by industrial methods

Energy flows where attention goes and when we've been too focused on the doing to communicate higher-level progress, confidence and engagement have dipped. We still have work to do in establishing consistent, autonomous feedback loops that keep the momentum alive.

Much of what we're building is still in its early, experimental stages and it is easy to default to a strategy set at the top by those who hold the overarching responsibility. But the real magic happens when departments are invited to interpret the mission for themselves, exploring what it means in their own context. That's when the spark catches: people light up, collaborate and use their unique gifts to bring their purpose to work. This is how a movement gains momentum, how it begins to shift the dial and change the collective mindset and how the butterfly effect unfolds.

We began to see our workplace, our new Schoolhouse, not as somewhere people were chained to computers but as a place of regenerative learning, as a space of culture and creativity, as a community where we could truly come together.

A few months later, in June 2022, we hosted our first Garden of Tomorrow festival, now an annual gathering. It quickly became a full team production, with every department bringing their unique gifts to create a grassroots event that showcased new stories of regenerative, Nature-integrated business to the wider business community.

We knew early on that, even though we were only just starting the journey ourselves, accelerating change would require bringing the SME community together. This was a time for cooperation; if we wanted to move the dial, we needed to make the journey together.

Beyond planting the seeds for change in the corporate world, the festival deeply activated our wider team. It gave them a meaningful contribution to shape, curate and produce – what the *Guardian* later called 'the most hopeful climate festival'.

We understood there could never be a cookie-cutter approach to any of this. Every business, every organisation carries its own unique conditions, size and culture. Each company is made up of a diverse group of people with different levels of awareness, connection and readiness.

But the one thing open to all of us – right where we are   is to begin to create the conditions.

The conditions for people to bring not just their labour but their creativity, intuition, care and purpose to work each day.

The conditions for teams to move from passive employees to active co-creators, ambassadors and stewards of something larger than any one of us.

The conditions for business to shift from extraction to regeneration – not as an abstract ideal but as a lived, imperfect, ongoing practice.

It wasn't about having all the answers or the perfect blueprint to follow. It was about learning to work like Nature itself: collaboratively, adaptively, in relationship and open to emergence.

Because when we change the conditions, we change the outcome.

And often we change the whole story.

CHAPTER 13

Mother Nature Is Hiring

'We do not inherit the earth from our ancestors,
we borrow it from our children.'

Old Proverb

September 2022 brought with it two pieces of news that marked a seismic shift in the story of business as usual.

British B Corp cosmetics brand Faith in Nature started the month with the news that they had become the first company in the world to legally appoint Mother Nature as a director, giving the living world a formal seat at the board table. When I read about in the *Guardian*, I thought that it was such was a radical and beautifully simple act, acknowledging what so many of us feel instinctively: that Nature has rights; that Nature has a voice and that businesses should be accountable to more than just humans.

It spoke to the very heart of what Javvy and I had been feeling as our relationship with Nature deepened and as She moved from being our design muse to becoming our teacher. This appointment was a mechanism to recognise that position and make Her voice official and legally binding.

Almost in the same breath, US brand Patagonia made global headlines. Founder Yvon Chouinard announced he was giving the company away and that all future profits would go towards protecting the planet because, as he put it, 'Earth is now our only shareholder.' The move was bold and unprecedented. Here was a company recognising the source of all wealth and protecting this life source. Once more in Yvon's words: 'Without a healthy environment, there are no shareholders, no employees, no customers, and no business.'

Both companies were rewriting the story of a company's relationship to Nature, showing us what it looks like when business is embedded in, and beholden to, the living world. These creative, out-of-the-box but entirely logical and legal acts were a reminder that we are Nature, and that our systems, our companies, our economies must begin to reflect that truth if we're to have any hope of a thriving future.

I found myself thinking more deeply about the rights of the natural world – and how strange and depressing that a company, a human-made entity on paper, can be granted rights, protections, even legal 'personhood', while a river that gives us water, a forest that gives us breath, the ocean that regulates our climate, the soil that feeds us, are seen as resources, commodities to be stripped rather than kin to be respected.

But change is rising. Across the world, activists, Indigenous leaders and visionary lawmakers are challenging this old paradigm. Legal personhood for Nature is beginning to take root. In countries such as New Zealand, Ecuador, Colombia and India, rivers and forests are being granted rights. Not as property, but as living beings, with voice, agency and standing. These shifts are not new ideas but ancient truths resurfacing, drawn from Indigenous worldviews that have never seen Nature as 'other' but as sacred kin. That recognition lives in my blood too. In the old Irish Brehon laws, the natural world was seen as sentient, the source of all life, and protected not merely for its utility, but for its sanctity. And now, in these urgent, emergent times, we are witnessing the return of this wisdom.

Learning about Faith in Nature's mechanism of putting Mother Nature on the board, devised by the visionary company directors behind it, Simeon and Anne Hopkins, in partnership with living-world lawyers Lawyers for Nature, truly blew my mind. Here was a living, legal blueprint for how to bring Nature's voice directly into a company, not as a symbolic gesture but as a structural safeguard. At this point, we were around six months into our own regenerative journey. It was gaining traction with our team, but this felt like a way to go beyond good intentions and truly take it beyond my and Javvy's advocacy of Nature protection; legally embedding the responsibility deep into the roots of House of Hackney and safeguarding its purpose for all future stewards of the brand. It would give everyone – at every level – the permission, duty and accountability to protect the very system we all depend on, not just for business but for life.

So, with a fire in my belly, I fired off an email to Lawyers for Nature, congratulating them on creating such a powerful, pioneering tool for bringing Nature's voice into business and asking whether they'd be open to working with us. The response from Brontie Ansell, the founder, co-creator of the mechanism and now the world's first Mother Nature director, was enthusiastic but also cautious. She was eager to see more champions of the model but was wary that the directorship could be adopted without integrity, that it could be diluted and used for marketing rather than authentic meaning. Tokenism and greenwashing are a legitimate concern, especially when the optics are attractive.*

We took Brontie through our journey and the importance we placed on Mother Nature – and how we wanted to honour the pivotal role She played. Not just as inspiration, but for Her life-giving contribution to our business: economically, ecologically, spiritually and creatively. As our mentor, muse, supplier, teacher, healer and guide. From the raw materials that shape our products to the seasonal cycles that shape our thinking, Nature is present in every thread, every colour, every

---

* A year later, Apple would release a high-production-value film featuring 'Mother Nature' as a character who quizzed their executives on climate progress. It was clever, polished and clearly designed to signal accountability, but for me, and others in the space, it rang a bit hollow and felt like a performance of sustainability rather than a true commitment to integrating Nature's voice in the company. And when you've got billions in cash reserves and a global supply chain, the bar of authenticity and integrity is higher. The danger is that symbolism without the substance behind it risks diluting the very movement it borrows from.

decision, not as an externality, but as the source of everything. We wanted to recognise this silent partner without whom there would be no House of Hackney.

It was time to make it official and bring Her voice into our decision-making. After extensive due diligence to ensure our motivations were sound, poring over our B Corp accreditation, holding meetings to authenticate both our journey to date and our future vision, we eventually passed the lawyers' rigorous litmus test. We had demonstrated our true intent and long-term commitment, and they agreed to guide us in creating a seat for Mother Nature *and* Future Generations on our board.

From the outset, we knew we'd need the buy-in from our private equity shareholders and we knew that wouldn't be easy. As anticipated, they weren't comfortable with the idea of giving Nature a vote and initially wanted the role to be observer only. But that didn't feel like it was enough – if the role was to have impact, we needed to give Mother Nature real agency. So, after a lot of negotiating and appealing to their humanity, reminding them of the importance of a role like this during a climate emergency, they finally agreed to the appointment of a non-executive director. While the role wouldn't carry full voting rights, there would be exceptional circumstances where, if over 75 per cent of the board approved, Mother Nature would get a vote. It wasn't perfect, but it was the first meaningful step. And we knew an exit was on the horizon in the next couple of years, at which point we could extend to a position that bestowed full voting powers to the directorship.

But even before that moment, we felt strongly that voting rights weren't the only marker of influence. We were a real-world example of a company operating with regular board constraints and needing to get to a place of compromise between parties. A non-voting Mother Nature directorship was still able to meaningfully guide and shape strategy and it ensured that in every key decision we made, across every department, the impact on Nature and human wellbeing was considered.

The very act of bringing the voices of Mother Nature and Future Generations into the boardroom – structurally, symbolically and strategically – catalysed a paradigm shift in how we saw Nature within our company. It changed the lens through which we made decisions and offered our team a reference point. It was a living daily reminder of what we are working in service of. It opened space for deeper questioning, greater integrity and a powerful sense of accountability beyond us as we asked ourselves the simple guiding question that Faith in Nature had conceived, '*What would Nature say?*' to help our daily decision-making.

And while the role began as advisory, it quickly proved just how much change could be seeded simply by giving Nature a consistent, independent voice. From strategy to supply chain to internal culture, the ripple effects in the company were undeniable. Because the Nature-representing director was empowered to seek independent advice from ecologists, Indigenous leaders, scientists and legal thinkers, it brought a depth and rigour to our decision-making that stretched far beyond our four walls. Whether or not she could vote, her presence changed everything.

Together with the company Articles, the role gave us full permission to charter the company in service of Nature. It pushed us not only to address our own supply chains, setting targets around materials and processes that restored more than they extracted, but also to invest time and resources into shaping a more responsible business model, one that integrated regeneration into its very design and could inspire others to follow. It also emboldened us to step beyond our own sector, backing our activism and enabling initiatives like the We Are Nature campaign to change the definition of 'Nature' in our dictionaries.

Brontie's Impact Report statement, published in June 2024 in response to the Impact Report, detailed two important points about the role:

The specifics of the representation of MN&FG [Mother Nature and Future Generations] are as follows, the rights holder is able to access all information needed to make sound decisions and influence policy. There is a financial budget for the rights holder to enable them to properly perform their duties. There is the right of participation in all key decision making spaces. There is the right of disclosure by all other stakeholders to inform and consult with the voices of MN&FG.

There is the right to time to gather valuable information and research in order for the rights holder to be fully informed.

In future the leadership also plans to look deeper at power sharing and veto options. There has also been a significant commitment to capital placement, capital flows and profit sharing by the board. The board does not fetter the voice or discretion of the holder of this position. Overall, this project has demonstrated that it is categorically possible to award rights to Nature in a meaningful and substantive way. The impact on the rights of nature trajectory should not be undervalued.

When the time came, after our private equity exit in 2025, we granted full voting rights to the role. It showed that that even within the constraints of conventional business, there is still room for radical action, for creativity and for meaningful change. And if we could do it, so could others, even within the confines of business ownership.

From my year of deep reading and immersion in Indigenous wisdom, the principle of 'seventh-generation thinking' stood out like a beacon to me. Rooted in Haudenosaunee philosophy, it calls on tribal leaders to consider the impact of their decisions on those born seven generations later as it asks a simple but profound question: will this decision serve the future life of the next 150 years? Will it be a gift or a burden for future generations? That lens of long-term stewardship felt like the exact antidote to the short-term thinking that dominates our systems today, especially in business. Most companies operate on three- to five-year plans with a laser focus on quarterly results and shareholder returns, without pausing to ask what will the ripple effect be in a few decades, let alone seven generations?

And it's no wonder. The UK Companies Act, the legislation that governs how businesses are run, was drafted in the late 1990s and early 2000s – an era with a very different awareness around Nature and the climate crisis. The Act's default mandate is short-term shareholder primacy. Section 172 briefly nods to employees, communities and the environment, but it doesn't hold directors legally accountable for those impacts, instead solely reinforcing their duty to promote the success of a company at all costs. There's no duty to think long term. It's essentially a rulebook that empowers directors to maximise financial return, not ecological integrity or intergenerational wellbeing.

But we're no longer living in the same world as when the Companies Act was created. We're in a climate emergency, and the rules and conventions need rewriting. That's why campaigns like the Better Business Act are so vital. Convened by B Lab UK and backed by a broad coalition of over two thousand businesses – from SMEs to household names like John Lewis, Iceland and Innocent – the Act calls for a simple but powerful change: to amend Section 172 of the Companies Act so that every business is legally required to advance the interests of people, planet and future generations alongside profit. The Act isn't about anti-growth or idealism but a heavy dose of realism in recognising that long-term prosperity depends on protecting the very foundations business relies on – natural resources, stable societies and healthy ecosystems.

So, the question became: how could we embed this kind of long-term mindset into House of Hackney? What would it look like to bring seventh-generation thinking into our governance – not just as a philosophy but as a decision-making structure?

It was my friend Satish Kumar, over lunch at Schumacher College, who first pointed me towards Wales. I had been telling him about our wish to bring future generations' thinking into our company. Wales was, and still is, the first and only country in the world to appoint a Future Generations Commissioner, a role enshrined in law through the Well-being of Future Generations Act (2015). This groundbreaking legislation requires all public bodies to consider the long-term impact of their decisions, not just on the next election cycle, but on the next century and beyond. Satish's friend Jane Davidson was the visionary behind the Act. After immersing myself in her book *#futuregen*, which explores how to make future-generations thinking real in government, and with an introduction from Satish, Sam, Kellie Brontie and I arranged to meet her.

We wanted her guidance on how to bring this kind of 'cathedral thinking': the ability to begin work on something you may never see completed but which will serve generations to come – into House of

Hackney. Our enquiry for Jane centred on some key questions: how to navigate the tension between short-term needs and long-term mission; how to land this kind of thinking with both our team and wider audiences, especially those not yet converted, and whether we should move beyond the three- to five-year traditional business plan and commit instead to a ten-year vision plan that could expand into more generational thinking.

What Jane told us was both grounding and galvanising. The work starts with a clear mission statement, she said, something everyone at every level understands and can get behind and quote – it's the anchor that allows actions to follow. She reminded us to focus on action because it is action that shifts behaviour and culture. And keep asking: *How is Nature improved by what we're doing?* In generational terms, a ten-year plan is not enough – twenty-five years is one generation, and a one-hundred-year vision, with shorter milestones nested within it, is what truly aligns a business with the future.

What struck me most in our conversation with Jane was the parallel between a small country and a small company. Both have the agility to experiment, to move quickly and to embed new paradigms. Jane showed us that long-term thinking wasn't just possible but transformative. Her work had helped shift the policy landscape of an entire nation, and it gave us the confidence that a company like ours could do the same.

So, we began weaving this thinking into our governance. It inspired us to extend the Mother Nature directorship we were in the process of creating to include Future Generations – to ensure that in every decision we make, we're considering the long-term consequences of our actions. We needed to imagine House of Hackney not just as a brand for now, but as a good ancestor of the future.

It led Javvy and me back into the ancient sequoia woods near Schumacher College to sit in silence with old trees and contemplate the big questions: what legacy could we leave? What is the purpose of our company in 150 years? The world didn't need another interiors brand when we launched twelve years previously, and it certainly won't need one in 150 years' time unless that brand is actively working to restore and be a good participant in life on Earth.

We defined a long-term purpose that would become our North Star:

*To reimagine business as a living system that restores the Earth, sparks creativity and protects the wellbeing of future generations.**

This purpose would become the litmus test for every shorter-term plan going forwards. In autumn 2023, we rewrote our company's Articles of Association, filed at Companies House, to reflect that Mother Nature and Future Generations were now directors of House of Hackney. To honour this milestone and help land the thinking, we gifted every team member a copy of the excellent *The Good Ancestor* by Roman Krznaric, a book that helped crystallise the paradigm shift we were making as a company. Much of what we were trying to introduce was so new, I didn't always have the language or the answers. I found that storytelling, and the right book, could go a long way in opening hearts and anchoring complex ideas. Often a story speaks louder than strategy.

Brontie Ansell, who originally pioneered the role at Faith in Nature, became the inaugural embodiment of the Mother Nature and Future Generations directorship at House of Hackney. Brontie brought rigour and provocation in equal measure. She wasn't here to rubber-stamp our progress; she was here to challenge, question and guide. She worked closely with senior leadership and individual departments, offering big ideas, sense-checking strategy and supporting us to move from doing 'less harm' to becoming truly regenerating ecosystems. She became a vital advocate for deepening each person's sense of agency in this collective journey.

That first year was a period of discovery, of pulling up the car bonnet and taking cold, clear-eyed looks at the changes we needed to make at every level to truly honour Nature as a stakeholder in everything we do.

And it was just the beginning.

---

* Our vision and mission statements are current iterations of the originals. The language has evolved over time, while the underlying intent and meaning remain the same.

As part of our move towards becoming a regenerative business, we created a new mission statement to guide our journey and make clear what we stand for:

House of Hackney is a restoration project rooted in Nature, Craft, Community and Awe! Inspired by Nature's living systems, we use creativity and business as catalysts to regenerate our common home.

We defined the company as a 'restoration project' to signify that we would use our agency and profits to restore Nature, our communities and ultimately ourselves. Restoration felt like the essential first step towards regeneration. We didn't want to just do less harm; we wanted to actively contribute to the healing of the living world.*

As part of the body of work to create the new directorship guided by Brontie, we also used the moment to revise our mission with a structural shift through the formal amendment of our company's Articles of Association. We changed our legal purpose at Companies House, enshrining our commitment not only to profit but to the protection and regeneration of Nature (including humans), for the quality of life of all future generations. After everything we'd been through with private equity, safeguarding our purpose in this way was a huge relief. It made our mission legally binding, not just for our stewardship of the brand but for its future guardians.

To help land the delivery of our new mission, Sam broke it down into three strategic pillars that would go on to form our regenerative roadmap:

---

* Around this time, the EU passed the Nature Restoration Law, an ambitious piece of legislation requiring member states to repair at least 20 per cent of land and sea by 2030. The act was a rare and encouraging moment of political alignment with planetary needs. This spirit of restoration, of cleaning up our world, mending what's been broken and committing to leave things better than how we found them, felt not just symbolic but urgent and necessary. Restoration was an important legitimate goal that needed our collective focus and action. It gave us confidence that our mission wasn't just idealistic; it was part of a wider cultural and ecological shift.

1. Nature Remuneration and Capital Flows: focused on how we manage and direct capital, asking how can our profits restore what's been extracted as a fund for regeneration?
2. Regeneration and Restoration: centred on transforming our greatest impacts, from the farms that grow our raw materials to the factory communities and the team who sell them, we ask how do we move from degenerative towards regenerative impact? Is it depleting or restoring?
3. Activism and Influence: championing creativity with purpose and using our voice and agency to share stories, challenges and solutions so that collectively we can shift the cultural narrative and rethink our place in Nature.

It's one thing to create a mission statement, but another to truly bake it into everyday actions. To make it real, we created tailored mission guidelines for every department, with litmus-test style questions and prompts designed to help guide decision-making in line with our purpose. There's no single right answer – we are all students on this journey – but the aim is to empower people to use their creativity and problem-solving skills to seek more responsible alternatives and create solutions and ways of doing in their roles. Every team member has goals and actions, often created by themselves, tied to the regenerative mission. This was key to making sure the work wasn't seen as additional but became fully embedded in our day to day and our culture.

As a product-making company, it was clear that our regenerative journey couldn't stop at just team culture or mission statements. We had to get to the root: our supply chain. Starting with our core categories of wallpaper, fabric and paint, we wanted to better understand the true cost of our products, not just the price we paid to the factories we worked with, but the hidden ecological and social toll embedded in every roll, every metre, every tin. It was something I'd been sitting with since that silent retreat in the woods on my fortieth birthday. What's the journey of a product to get here? What's the story behind the material, the labour, the land?

If we were to create heirloom products that honour future generations, we needed to design for longevity, circularity and stewardship, looking at every input and stage from raw material to end-of-life. So, we kicked off a three-year innovation programme with our core suppliers to accelerate material shifts, moving to regenerative cotton and fossil-free paint ingredients and even exploring forest-free wallpaper. Across our wider business, we started to trial material alternatives using fungi, microbes and agricultural waste, using more restorative materials to contribute to the wellbeing of Nature, not just our bottom line.

As we started to dive deeper into our product impact, it became clear that to create real change we'd have to go beyond just our business. We were just one small company. Our factories were small, too, with limited buying power in the grand scheme of things. To reach the roots – the growing of the fibres, the raw materials, the manufacturing processes – we'd need to get to the source, to the raw materials industry. And that meant bringing our supply chain with our key industries of paper, cotton and paint together. It meant gathering suppliers together who, on paper, were competitors, and collectively looking at how we could reimagine the system, not through the lens of competition but through the lens of cooperation. Because if we were serious about systemic change, about shifting entire categories like wallpaper, fabric and paint towards regeneration, we had to work together.

So, we began hosting an annual supplier summit at Trematon, gathering key players across the interiors industry and supply base. What emerged was powerful: companies who were once rivals openly sharing ideas, concerns, challenges and breakthroughs, united by the shared aim of safeguarding the future. Together, we started setting collective targets: to find a solution for tree-free wallpaper using agricultural waste, to switch from conventional to regenerative cotton, to pioneer a plant-based paint binder that would eliminate reliance on fossil-fuel derivatives and reduce harmful VOC emissions and, crucially, to open-source the whole process. Even if we'd done a lot of the leg work. Because the goal wasn't competitive advantage. It was transformation. And transformation is a team sport.

This journey has made me think deeply about beauty – and how our perception of beauty in a product needs to move beyond the surface: to how it was made, whether its process caused harm and how long it will last. As we make tougher decisions around products and materials, I can already see the aesthetic we're known for beginning to change – and it's one I'm excited to embrace. As an example, as we move from conventional to organic velvet, its gentle 'grinning', those little creases that appear when it becomes a cushion, carries a character that conventional velvet with its superficial perfection simply cannot match. It is like the beauty and character of laughter lines and smiling eyes on an older face. We will continue to redefine beauty as something that goes far beyond skin-deep.

Alongside our deep-dive into product, we knew that if we were truly going to walk the talk, the journey to becoming regenerative would mean pulling away from partnerships and collaborations where we weren't in control of the supply chain. In these transitional times, the challenge was to keep the lights on: to maintain financial and team stability as we moved from business as usual towards transformational change. One of the first big steps was to progress away from collaborations with major retailers whose production values hadn't evolved enough to align with ours. Around that time, a seven-figure partnership offer came in from an airline. Without much sleep lost, we politely declined. And for other longstanding partnerships already in motion, even ones we relied on financially, we followed our intuition and chose to walk away. These decisions instantly whacked our bottom line. But we now had to review everything through a lens of what served Nature and what no longer did, and what we had to compost in the hope of making space for something new to emerge. It was galvanising but it wasn't easy.

Choosing this path meant choosing uncertainty over anything we could predict, letting go of the safe, profitable partnerships that kept us financially secure and saying no to offers that once would've felt like a bonus. There were many moments of self-doubt. What if we were too early? Too radical? But in those moments, I took confidence from the belief that we were building something rooted in the principles of Nature's living systems – and with the right conditions, those systems have never failed. They bring and enhance life. But it took a degree of blind faith to trust that we were clearing space for something more in service to our purpose to grow. At this stage, we were only putting the conditions in place, and that often felt scary. But, then again, there's nothing that tells you that hydrogen and oxygen, when brought together under the right conditions, will create something as magical and life-giving as water. So, we had to trust in our vocation, in our intuition and in the model of life itself.

After a year of helping to get us on our way, guiding us through the pivotal transition from intention to implementation, sense-checking our strategy, laying foundations and holding us to account with some tough love when we needed it – it felt like we were in good stead. Like some sort of Mother Nature Mary Poppins, Brontie had swooped in, helped us find our feet, and when the wind changed, it was time for her to move on. But before she left, speaking in the voice of Mother Nature, she issued us with the invitation of our times:

Birth a business model that honours Nature as a stakeholder. One that protects more than it takes, and begins to repair not only our own footprint, but the legacy damage left by generations before us, so that those yet to come still have the chance to live on a thriving, beautiful planet.

When it came time to find Brontie's successor, our call for applicants, 'Mother Nature is hiring', became the most responded-to ad we've ever run. Something about the role – equal parts visionary, activist, guardian and provocateur – struck a deep chord with people. We were inundated with applications from an extraordinary mix of people: ecologists, lawyers, artists, strategists, poets. It was an incredibly tough decision but, in the end, the role went to Charmian Love, a powerful voice in the movement for business as a force for good. The process introduced us to a brilliant extended network of experts we continue to learn from and collaborate with today.

For this next stage – answering the challenge to birth a new business model that honours Nature – we needed someone with a deep understanding of systems thinking. With Charmian's experience as co-founder of B Lab UK, and her work with Natura & Co, one of the world's leading B Corps pioneering regenerative practices at scale across beauty, people and planet, she felt like the perfect embodiment of the role. At Natura, already further along on their journey towards regeneration, they had begun shaping strategies that were grounded in interconnectedness and were showing proof of concept that a global business can align with the wellbeing of ecosystems and communities. That's exactly the kind of leadership that would help us evolve. Where Brontie helped us root the role of Nature within the foundations of our company, Charmian arrived to help grow the canopy, to stretch its reach, deepen its roots and bring others into the shade of this emerging model.

What we were missing, we came to realise, was not intent but a decision-making compass – a clear litmus test that could guide choices at board level when trade-offs were complex and the path sometimes unclear.

Through our conversations with Charmian, we began to articulate what she was already busy architecting behind the scenes: a way of asking not 'Is this legal?' or 'Is this profitable?' but 'Would Mother Nature support this decision?'

From this question emerged what we came to call the Mother Nature Going Concern Test – a reworking of an accounting concept normally used to judge financial viability, expanded to encompass ecological and social legitimacy.

In essence, Mother Nature will support a business (or a business decision within) so long as certain conditions are being met, which are:

- The business actively builds awareness of, and connection to, the natural world.
- The business supports the wellbeing of its people, recognising human health as inseparable from planetary health.
- The business measures its full externalities, both positive and negative, across natural, social and human capital.
- The business takes meaningful action to reduce harm, prioritising reduction and insetting (fixing impacts at source) rather than offsetting wherever possible.
- The business articulates a clear vision for what a truly regenerative business model would look like, even if it cannot yet fully inhabit it.

- The cost of transitioning to this regenerative model is treated as a long-term investment, recognised on the balance sheet and depreciated over time, rather than hidden or deferred.
- The business practises radical transparency, sharing learnings, data and – where possible – intellectual property, in service of collective progress.
- The business actively backs system-changing initiatives designed to protect Mother Nature, including campaigns for ecocide law, the Climate and Nature Bill, and the Better Business Act.

Together, these conditions reframed our understanding of what it means to be a *going concern* – not merely financially solvent, but legitimate in the eyes of the living system on which all business depends.

Because a Mother Nature directorship isn't just a role. It's a revolution in how we think about governance, responsibility and legacy. The systems we inherited were never designed to serve all of life. But we can design better ones.

Mother Nature isn't just hiring at House of Hackney. She's hiring everywhere. And the role is open to all who are ready to reimagine business not as extraction but as restoration. Not as ownership but as participatory stewardship.

CHAPTER 14

We Are Nature

'The greatest group noun of them all: the entangled web of planetary life of which humans are a part.'

Robert Macfarlane, a definition of Nature
in support of our We Are Nature campaign

The wondrous effects of Nature on us aren't so surprising – because we *are* Nature. Not separate from it. Not visitors to it. Not above it. No different, fundamentally, from the trees or birds or rivers, whose canopy, root and tributary systems are mirrored in our lungs and veins. And if ever there was doubt, we can stare at our thumbprint, whose imprint echoes the rings of a tree, as no greater living proof that we are kin, as surely as we resemble a family member.

We are meant to be together, intricately and symbiotically connected, dancing the miracle of exchange, our out-breath of carbon dioxide becoming the trees' in-breath, and their exhale of oxygen becoming our life force. So, as the Nature creatures that we are, it makes perfect sense that we feel more embodied and nourished when we return to the environments we were made for. And the opposite is equally true – being separated from Nature in our daily lives is costing us.

It wasn't supposed to be this way. When the first machines arrived, they brought promises of freedom. The Industrial Revolution promised liberation – that with its gifts of steam and steel, we would be freed from toil, bestowed with leisure and finally have time to enjoy the fruits of our labour. We would have time to spend with our families;

time to daydream in the fields and feel time slow under the open sky. And when the Digital Age dawned, it promised that life would become effortless, automated, frictionless, with computers in the palms of our hands and smart homes at our fingertips, shielding us from the seasons. We were sold that the more advanced life would become, the more time we'd have to actually live it.

But the opposite has happened. Instead of freedom, we have become at best imprisoned by the very modern constructs we've created, and at worst enslaved to a version of capitalism that values productivity over presence. And now, as we enter the age of artificial intelligence, we see this same reductionist mindset accelerating. Unless we fundamentally shift the assumptions beneath it, AI won't be used to liberate us for more meaningful work, as we've been promised. Instead of freeing us to focus on creativity, care or community, its real application will be to reduce labour costs, increase margins and further enrich the few, all while continuing to treat humans as units of output: disposable, replaceable and dehumanised. And in doing so, we risk becoming even more disconnected from the meaning and purpose of our own existence.

Our physiology has not evolved as quickly as the so-called signs of progress. We are not built for this pace, this enclosure, this distance from the living world. Our indoor life ignores the fact that biologically we need sunlight, fresh air, fingers in the soil, movement and stillness as much as we need food or water. We have forgotten that our cells still sing with pleasure and awe when touched by the wildness of the world. The pace of so-called progress has accelerated beyond what our bodies and spirits can endure. We are living in an age of unprecedented disconnection from the natural world.

And it has happened within just a few generations.

For most of human history, we lived embedded in ecosystems that were in harmony with Nature: hunting, growing, gathering in our tribes, highly attuned to the cycles and seasons. But in the past two hundred years, and even more so in the past twenty, we have been summoned indoors. Schools, offices, homes, transport, even play and social life have become mostly interior experiences. We've put up too many walls between Nature and ourselves. Nature is now something we visit, not something we live within.

The impact over this short period of time has been profound.

It's not surprising that we are sicker, lonelier and more anxious and depressed than ever before. We have forgotten the names of the trees to pass down to the next generations. We have swapped our child-hoods spent climbing trees and having outdoor adventures for ones spent in virtual adventures in the Metaverse. I weep for our children who are growing up with fewer hours outside than prisoners, more familiar with emojis than animal tracks, more fluent in touchscreen gestures than in the language of the wild, losing their sensory intel-ligence, their resilience, their joy with this shift indoors. Has 'the last child in the woods', in Richard Louv's words, already bolted? We have normalised a way of being that goes against our biology. The way we work today – indoors, under artificial light, sedentary for hours in front of screens, disengaged from natural rhythms in our lives – is a product of a late capitalist system that prioritises productivity over wellbeing. It's leaving us disembodied, *dis-at-ease*. It's quite literally diseasing us.

———

Through our seasonal initiatives – summer's long weekends and win-ter's gentle hours – we started to witness early on a transformation in our team. For a London-based team with access to Nature often out of reach, it was beautiful to see how many began to carve out time for Nature. They'd arrive on Monday mornings after a long weekend outdoors, all wind-kissed faces and a new aliveness in their eyes.

It turned out to be a win-win. Although our primary metrics of suc-cess for these circadian honouring initiatives were around wellbeing, there was a ripple effect of improved productivity, stronger retention and even better sales. The numbers followed the people.

We came to understand early on that a team connected to Nature would be more engaged in considering the impact of their day-to-day decisions on the natural world. This, in turn, accelerated the essential shifts we needed to make, pivoting towards materials, processes and systems that honoured Nature's living systems and principles.

I began to notice how they carried this advocacy for Nature into their choices and conversations with each other, with suppliers and customers, and within their wider circles of influence as they started to became ambassadors for regeneration.

As our mission to become a regenerative company deepened, this kind of thinking became even more essential. Regeneration isn't just about the planet – it begins with people. A team connected to Nature will want to protect Her more fiercely.

We knew then that if we gave even more time back in Nature, our team would forge even deeper, more personal relationships with it. And deeper connection leads to deeper care.

In 2025, the success of the programme, and the abundant upsides it brought, gave us the confidence to roll out a four-day week all year round. So, we launched Nature Fridays, an extra day each week for our team to spend in Nature, on their own terms and with the same salary. Some greet the sun. Some volunteer with community growing projects. Some walk, draw, swim, run or simply just be in the wild. It's about building on each person's unique relationship with the natural world.*

In order to be able to give back the extra fifty-odd days to our team each year, while hitting our business goals and maintaining holistic business health, we had to set ourselves up for working less, but smarter. That meant becoming laser focused on the objectives. We place a high importance on thoughtful goal setting, workflow planning and communication. These rhythms and structures keep our house in order and give us the gift of time.

---

* The latest UK trial of a four-day week, conducted in late 2024 and early 2025, involved seventeen companies and all have decided to keep the four-day week permanently. Without being specifically Nature-focused, nearly one thousand employees now enjoy shorter weeks without sacrificing salary, reporting less burnout, better mental health and greater life satisfaction. The earlier 2022 UK landmark pilot involving sixty-one organisations [around three thousand people] saw 92 per cent of companies continue with the model, along with improved productivity, 35 per cent revenue growth and a 57 per cent drop in attrition. With results like this I envisage the four-day week becoming standard practice over the next decade.

But at the heart of it all is trust in each team member to play their part in the holistic health of the company, empowering them with the autonomy to do it in a way that works best for them. We've also invested in streamlining our backend systems so that we can automate the mundane and our talented team can focus on what they do best: using their creativity to move our mission forwards.

Nature Fridays became part of a broader initiative to spend more time with Nature during the working week. While the four-day week was a powerful step forwards for Nature connection and health, we were still uneasy about spending four days indoors – sedentary and disconnected from the rhythms that nourish us. We knew we needed more than long weekends to get our dose of Nature, we needed access to be woven into our everyday lives. Since the workday takes up the majority of our waking hours, it was clear that we needed to shake this up.

So, we introduced a Time With Nature policy to encourage the team to spend time outside during the workday. We placed autonomy at the centre of it, trusting people to make choices that would balance their own wellbeing with the needs of the business. When could a small meeting become a walking meeting? Could a larger one be held outdoors? Could Wednesday's protected flow time when meetings were exchanged for focus happen outside? The answer was almost always a resounding yes. Yes, it might take a little more planning, and we'd need to be more reactive to the weather and come prepared with the right clothes, equipment and tools. But the trade-offs and pay-offs were always more than worth any perceived effort.

In my little makeshift outdoor offices, I learned early on, or perhaps it was more like I remembered, that being in Nature brings out the most creative thinking, something I had subconsciously known as a child in the garden building imaginary worlds. Nature activates us. It enhances our creative flow, expands our perspective and helps us land ideas and solutions with much greater clarity. My best creative downloads have always come when I've been in Nature. And science backs this too: time in Nature increases our divergent thinking,

When we moved into St Michael's, our London HQ, a former clergy house with an old schoolhouse attached that now serves as our head office, we gained an internal courtyard. We filled it with café tables and chairs, with easy access to battery packs, blankets and hot water bottles for cooler days. It's become an important doorway to the outdoors during our working days.

Kellie, our head of regeneration, painstakingly mapped every accessible green space – parks, gardens, cemeteries – within our square mile in the City of London, creating a living guide for wandering minds and walking meetings.

The Time With Nature initiative has made for a more creative, resilient, solution-oriented team. When we align ourselves with the natural world, we tap into the same generative life force that Nature has always gifted us – and the creativity to imagine, to build and to regenerate.

And yet, this feels like just the beginning.

In a not-too-distant future I'd love for us, we will begin our workdays outside in the community garden we're slowly breathing back to life. I picture it inspired by the daily morning meetings at Schumacher College, which I've been lucky enough to witness many times, gathering in Nature to start the day as we share our plans; perhaps a thought, a poem or a simple creative exercise to honour the spirit of the day, energise our company community and bring a touch of the sacred into our working lives.

Freed from the constraints of private equity, and with Mother Nature now having a vote, we can now take our board meetings outside, too. Only then is Nature truly represented at the table. Let's normalise gathering under trees. We often speak about inviting Nature *in* to the boardroom, but what if, all along, She is inviting us *outside* instead?

Yes, there will be awkwardness. We've been so indoctrinated that we've been taught to believe that sitting at a desk is the only place where the real work happens. So, at first, it will feel unfamiliar. And there will likely be resistance to stepping outside the usual ways of working. But, as we allow the natural light in both literally and metaphorically, with each small step, people quickly begin to feel the difference. They feel better. Their energy lifts. They cope more easily. They're happier. They're more alive. And that's the turning point. Because humans don't just respond to logic but to how something makes us feel. When people experience the benefits in their own bodies, it no longer feels like an abstract idea or a policy shift. It becomes something they want to protect, and something they begin to champion themselves.

And the benefits ripple outwardly and exponentially. The company becomes more resilient, more creative, more focused. Teams become more collaborative, more present, more connected because when people are thriving, the culture thrives too. If the greatest outcome of our little corner of work here at House of Hackney is that fifty or so people develop a deeper relationship with Nature, feel better in themselves and begin to activate their influence to protect the Earth, then that's a result I'm deeply proud of.

It's come full circle, though. The daughter, who once in utero guided me back towards the earth, now spends most of her day indoors within the constructs of the school day. We often find ourselves in a quiet tug-of-war over screen time. She's developed a kind of selective amnesia of the deep, instinctual wisdom she once carried so fiercely, the same wisdom that urged me to put down my tech and step outside. Now, it's my responsibility to help her remember, to guide her back to the knowing that still lives inside her.

If we're to truly align our future with Nature, we need to look beyond the workplace and into our schools. Because children are hardwired to commune with the living world, not to be raised apart from it. They deserve school days that truly honour their natural rhythms. Days with space to move, rest, breathe and connect with the living world around them.

We've seen firsthand how instinctual that connection can be, when we worked with three Hackney schools on the We Are Nature campaign. Kids don't need convincing. They already know they are Nature. And Nature-connected children grow into Earth-protecting adults.

That project grew into something far larger than we imagined.

———

In 2023, I found myself inside the rainforest biodome at the Eden Project in Cornwall, attending a workshop at the Anthropy conference on the theme of Nature connection. Anthropy, founded by John O'Brien in 2022 as a response to the need for fresh leadership thinking, brings together leaders, thinkers and change-makers from across business, culture and civil society, all with the shared aim of reimagining Britain's future. As we sat in circle, surrounded by towering palms and the hum of unseen insects, the facilitator stood, cleared her throat and read aloud the *Oxford English Dictionary* definition of 'Nature'. What followed was a jolt – a definition so narrow and outdated it felt almost absurd in that lush, breathing space.

The phenomena of the physical world collectively; esp. plants, animals, and other features and products of the earth itself, **as opposed to humans.**

We were stopped in our tracks. There it was, in black and white, in the bastion of the English language, the declaration that humans were not part of Nature. Hearing it felt like being told we were not part of our own family. First came silence, then a deep, almost physical wave of sadness – a grief that seemed to settle over the whole circle.

Back in London a few days later, I shared the discovery in our Nature directorship planning meeting, where we were working alongside the law firm Lawyers for Nature to create the required legal accountability frameworks and defining what 'Nature' and 'Future Generations' meant. What we discovered devastated us. Humans were currently excluded from the definition of Nature as a noun in **all** major English dictionaries.

Language itself was reinforcing the illusion of separation, the very illusion that has enabled so much destruction. We soon learned that dictionaries don't invent meaning; they reflect it, mirroring the dominant beliefs of the time. And for centuries, the prevailing worldview in the Global North has been shaped by a worldview of separation – that humans were apart from and superior to Nature.

But that worldview is beginning to shift as science affirms what many Indigenous cultures have always known – that we are biologically, spiritually and ecologically entwined with the living world. Trees, we now know, communicate through underground mycorrhizal networks, exchanging nutrients, sending warnings and supporting one another in ways once dismissed as mythic but now proven by science. Our

DNA is deeply shared with our Earth cousins – we carry 99 per cent of the same genetic material as chimpanzees, 60 per cent as bananas and even 50 per cent as fungi! Our internal clocks are shaped by the same circadian rhythms that all of Nature runs on, regulating everything from our sleep to metabolism and impacting our immunity and mood, reminding us that our biology is calibrated to the Earth's pulse. And yet, our language still lags behind.

Robin Wall Kimmerer calls it 'the it-ing of Nature', this habit in English of reducing all that is alive and sentient to an inert object. Others have named it the 'thingification' of Nature. Once something becomes an 'it', a thing, it can be possessed, exploited or discarded. Our grammar conspires with our culture to sever the bonds of kinship.

For me, this has become impossible to ignore. My fingers recoil now if I try to type 'it' for Mother Nature. I can't bring myself to call Her a thing. That's why, throughout this book, you've seen me writing 'Her' instead. It doesn't yet feel fully fluent – sometimes I stumble, sometimes I hesitate – but it feels much closer to the truth. Language shapes how we see and how we act. To move beyond the thingification of Nature, we must begin with our words. To change our relationship with Her, we must first change the way we speak of Her.

Dictionaries carry immense responsibility. More than just repositories of meaning, they are mirrors of culture and shape how we think, teach, legislate and live. In the English-speaking world, UK dictionaries, especially the *Oxford English Dictionary*, are often the gold standard – consulted in classrooms, courts and parliaments alike. Seen as the final arbiters of meaning, they hold the power to define not just words, but outcomes.

When the most trusted reference texts define Nature in opposition to humanity, they reinforce a damaging illusion of separation. This linguistic divide, no matter how subtle, has real-life consequences. Because if we believe we are outside of Nature, it becomes easier to justify harming it. But if we remember that we are made of the same matter and held by the same systems, our choices begin to shift. Our relationship begins to repair.

My co-pilot on the campaign was Jessie Mond Wedd, a brilliant barrister from Lawyers for Nature who happened to be a close friend. She grew up in a household shaped by environmental leadership and public service: her father, Peter Melchett, spent decades at the forefront of environmental campaigning, progressive politics and sustainable agriculture, including working with Greenpeace and the Soil Association.

Together, we recognised that the prevailing English-language definitions of 'Nature' were born in a different era and no longer reflected the values or understanding of today's society. With an emerging worldview – and growing scientific evidence – the human-excluding definition had become increasingly out of step and in need of an accurate update. We felt compelled to act.

So, we pooled our skills: the creative legal minds of Lawyers for Nature alongside our own work in storytelling and culture. From this partnership, the We Are Nature campaign was born, with the goal of changing the definition of 'Nature' to include humans. Our longer-term aim was to help reclaim our place within the natural world, foster a deeper sense of interconnectedness, and ultimately support greater societal and planetary wellbeing. Because the *Oxford English Dictionary* definition had been the original catalyst, we decided to present our case directly to them.

Before we approached them, we first sought feedback on how 'Nature' should be defined. Nature thrives on collaboration, so we invited a mix of academics, creatives and activists, and kids from three Hackney schools to share their own definitions. Their responses unanimously included humans within Nature. These results confirmed that the current definition no longer reflected our evolving worldview – or the evidence.

When we then researched the dictionary entry itself, we struck gold. Behind a paywall, we found a wider definition that explicitly included human beings:

In a wider sense: the whole of the natural world, including human beings; the cosmos.

The initial excitement quickly faded when we saw that this definition had been marked 'obsolete'. Yet its presence mattered. It showed there was already a lexicographical precedent for understanding humans as part of Nature.

Alongside the crowdsourced definitions, we challenged this classification with evidence of continued usage. In response, the *Oxford English Dictionary* removed the word 'obsolete', made the entire entry freely accessible and committed to keeping the definition under review as language continues to evolve.

But beyond the dictionary definition, and perhaps just as importantly, the campaign catalysed a national conversation in the UK, around our kitchen tables, in our classrooms and across the media, about our place in Nature.

A year later, on Earth Day 2025, we expanded the campaign to every major English-language dictionary with a focus on the US dictionaries including Merriam-Webster, Dictionary.com and more. It quickly gained support from environmental stalwarts like Robin Wall Kimmerer, Joanna Macy and Janine Benyus, whose voices were rooted in Indigenous wisdom, systems change and biomimicry. These women had originally taught me so much about our kinship with Nature and they brought both inspiration and intellectual depth to the campaign.

As part of the evidence we presented, we showed that even AI language models, trained on vast and diverse human-created text, were already unanimously describing Nature in holistic terms, with humans inseparable from the web of life. This was significant: these models do not invent meaning but reflect the dominant patterns in our collective language use. The fact that they were already mirroring a worldview of interconnectedness suggested that culture itself was shifting – our language was evolving back to the truth of our belonging. And the dictionaries need to evolve theirs.

By the time of writing in August 2025, Dictionary.com had confirmed it was reviewing its own entry, using the case we had presented. We'll keep sharing the updated evidence with them, but dictionaries are slow-moving beasts – even with the *OED* precedent.

———

We Are Nature was an example of spreading a new story – the real story – where language is updated to place us back within our home in Nature's realm. The story resonated not only because it was true, but because it was delivered through the human creativity of our story-tellers: our artists and designers, our copywriters, photographers and filmmakers. When creativity is fused with purpose, it has the power to shift the cultural narrative faster than any policy or politics. The campaign moved people through the medium of storytelling and the power of enchantment. It was a reminder that it is within our realm to create new stories, to use our gifts as narrative beings – not only to tell stories, but to reshape them through the vessels of art and language. In the same way, scratch beneath the surface of one of our collections and a wallpaper is never just a wallpaper, but a creation with a unique story to tell, a purpose to serve and a heart to move.

This belief – that creativity fused with purpose can transform the world – is also what led us to launch, in 2025, a bursary for young artists and makers in partnership with the William Morris Gallery and IntoUniversity. Together, we are creating the William Morris Art Futures Bursary, supporting sixteen- to twenty-five-year-olds from Hackney and Waltham Forest – areas rich in cultural heritage but facing deep economic inequalities – to access art education, mentorship and creative opportunity.

It is a fund for young people brimming with imagination and talent, who might not otherwise have access to the materials, training or guidance needed to pursue their dreams. Inspired by the values of William Morris – art for all, meaningful work and the transformative power of creativity – the bursary seeks to nurture the next generation of artists and makers from two of London's most culturally vibrant yet economically marginalised boroughs.

At a time when art and craft education has been steadily rolled back in schools, sacrificed in favour of STEM subjects, the bursary feels more vital than ever. We are in a moment where the world needs storytellers, dreamers and makers of meaning as much as it needs scientists and coders. We need to support our artistic intelligence, not just the artificial one, remembering that it is our human creativity – our imagination, intuition and ability to make beauty from raw materials – that is unique to us as a species. To nurture these gifts is not a luxury but our birthright, and a necessity for culture, community and the future of life on Earth.

Above all, we want to raise awareness of art and crafts as valuable and viable career paths and create a scalable, community-rooted model that can grow in future years with wider support and reclaim the idea of arts and crafts as something purposeful and beautiful. Art has the power to move. Art speaks to our uniquely human gifts. And our hope is that by investing in young artists and makers, we are not only nurturing individual gifts but seeding the cultural and creative future of our community.

Because it's initiatives like this that remind us why we are in the business of creating and selling. Somewhere along the way, a certain kind of capitalism gave business a bad name. But profit, at its best, is energy. It is meant to move, to circulate, to feed life. And when that energy flows towards creativity, community and Nature, it generates the greatest return of all. We can do great things with profit.

William Morris understood this instinctively. Through his company, he proved that business and beauty can coexist – that commerce can be a conduit for purpose, not just an end in itself. In many ways, Morris & Co. was a manifesto disguised as a business. And that is endlessly inspiring to us at House of Hackney – to use creativity as a tool for change, for connection and for shared meaning.

———

What we believe about our place in Nature determines how we perceive, value, shape and interact with it. How we live with Nature now will determine our future and that of all life on earth. We are the first generations to really know about climate change and the last to be able to make a real difference. In a world of interconnectedness every action has a reaction. Failure to acknowledge this, and our dependence on Nature, will have far-reaching consequences.

It's up to us now to create the conditions for reconnection and in the process reorient our workplaces, schools and cities to honour this biological belonging to the Earth.

But this shift goes beyond working hours. It's about designing lives that honour our bond with the Earth. What if guaranteed time with Nature was built into every week – not as a perk but as a basic human right?

Because when we remember our place in the living world, protection becomes instinct. Being in Nature isn't a luxury: it's a homecoming. It is our birthright.

This isn't about slowing down for its own sake. It's about waking up again and returning to what is true: that we are not machines, but ecosystems. And as ecosystems, we thrive when we are in relationship.

It starts with how we shape our everyday. How we raise our children. How we work, how we gather, how we speak of Nature, and how we see our veins reflected in Her rings and roots. Now we need the courage to live it. To remember the ancient truth: we are, and have always been, Nature.

CHAPTER 15

Wake Up and Smell the Roses

'And then the day came when the risk to remain tight in a bud was more painful than the risk it took to blossom.'

Elizabeth Appell, 'Risk'

Nowhere is our distortion of value more devastating than in how we perceive Nature and how we fail to value Her within our economies and businesses. We draw on Nature's imagery for branding, use Her metaphors to sell things and depend on Her resources to power every part of our economy. And yet, we fail to account for Her in the very systems that define economic success.

Nature doesn't appear on the balance sheet. Her losses aren't recorded in the profit and loss: Her forests, rivers, wetlands, pollinators and climate systems are rendered invisible unless they can be commodified. Unless they can be bought, sold or extracted from. This is the ultimate failure of our metrics: we are erasing the very life systems we depend on and calling it progress.

When the *Dasgupta Review* first made headlines in 2021, I skimmed the coverage but filed it away in the 'important but abstract' part of my brain. It wasn't until 2023 when Kellie shared the *New York Times'* short film synopsis of the report, *An Actor, an Economist and the Answer to Everything* with the management team that its urgency truly landed. Commissioned by the UK's Treasury and led by Cambridge economist Sir Partha Dasgupta, the 600-page review was a sweeping examination of the economics of biodiversity, arguing that our economies are embedded within Nature, not external to it, and that our failure to account for the depletion of natural capital is a profound and life-critical design flaw. The NYT video distilled this complexity into five unforgettable minutes, anchored by Partha's clarity and the actor Alexander Skarsgård's charm, using metaphors and visuals to make the point that if we don't put Nature on the balance sheet, we are blind to our real losses. The video uses vivid, easy-to-grasp analogies to show how incomplete our economic scorekeeping really is:'Imagine a team that only measures its success by the goals it scores and ignores the goals it concedes,' Partha explains. 'That team could be losing the whole game without even realising it.'

It all boiled down to one simple truth: we need to pay for what we use. Take the example of chicken. A cheap, factory-farmed chicken is far more affordable than an organic one, yet its true ecological cost never makes it onto the price tag. Intensive poultry operations are polluting rivers with phosphorus runoff, degrading ecosystems and harming the very communities who live along their banks in the production process. When we buy a carton of orange juice, we're not paying for the value of the pollinators lost to pesticides. Without accounting for this immense loss to life, these hidden costs stay invisible. To paraphrase Partha, we keep telling ourselves we're winning – when we're losing the match that matters most.

The *Dasgupta Review* called for a fundamental reimagining of our economic models to one that places Nature at the centre, not at the margins. Watching the film around our boardroom table that afternoon confirmed what we had been intuitively feeling – that our current economic model is not only inadequate but also suicidal, as we are liquidating our life support systems to feed a fiction of growth at all costs. It was clear that we needed a radical redesign of how we define value, make decisions and measure success in our businesses. So, when our Mother Nature and Future Generations director formally briefed us to do just that, we knew we had no choice but to try.

We wondered if a model or a blueprint already existed. Were there businesses out there already placing a real value on Nature, not as an offset or a cost to be minimised, but as a living system whose protection is non-negotiable? Were there companies where profit is not the sole end goal, but a means to honour and regenerate the Earth? Were there businesses that had moved beyond the reductionist lens of valuing success as profit alone and towards valuing the holism of thriving ecosystems? And were they measuring this success in the health, vitality and resilience of the whole?

Before we could redesign how value was defined, we went looking for the models that had tried to do it before us. One of the most influential was the 'triple bottom line' – a framework of the three Ps: people, planet and profit, born in the 1990s of sustainability pioneer John Elkington, often called the 'godfather of corporate responsibility'.

His provocation was radical for its time: companies should measure not just profit, but also their impact on people and planet. It was a challenge to shareholder primacy and an invitation to embrace stakeholder wellbeing – a step towards reframing success beyond the purely financial. But decades later, Elkington himself issued what he called a 'recall' of the concept. In 2018, he admitted the triple bottom line had been 'captured and diluted' by the very corporations it sought to reform. Profit remained the dominant metric, while people and planet were tacked on like accessories instead of being fully integrated into a redefinition of value itself.

In 2006, after being popularised by the UN Principles for Responsible Investment, environmental, social and governance (ESG) frameworks started to emerge as they offered a path for capital markets to assess environmental and social performance alongside governance practices. For the first time, sustainability began to enter the language of investors. But the framing was telling – Nature and society were cast primarily as risks or opportunities to financial returns and not as living systems with their own intrinsic value.

But neither the triple bottom line nor ESG treated Nature as what it truly is. The 'P' of profit still outweighed the other two Ps of people and planet. Nature remained an 'externality', something to be managed, mitigated or offset, rather than recognised as the living foundation without which there is no economy at all.

For us, with Mother Nature now so visible in our company, this rang painfully true. Business was still measuring the wrong things

– and through far too narrow a lens. What was missing wasn't just stronger ESG reporting or more ambitious carbon targets. What was missing was *Nature*. And if we weren't finding a deep enough framework that truly placed Nature on our balance sheet, then we needed to build it ourselves.

The *Dasgupta Review* lit the path. We needed to start by identifying the *true* cost of our price – the hidden ecological and societal debts embedded in every product we make. Costs no one pays for at checkout, yet Nature always bears.

I first encountered a glimpse of this in 2021 at a B Corp festival in Amsterdam, during a presentation about a pioneering experiment in the Netherlands. The grocery store De Aanzet had become the first in the world to display two prices for selected products: the conventional market price, and a 'true price' that accounted for the hidden social and environmental costs: carbon emissions, underpaid labour, water use, land degradation. Shoppers could choose either price, with the difference going to projects that repaired those harms.

The experiment, led by the True Price Foundation, really hit home. Many customers willingly paid the higher true price – not from obligation, but a desire to align their purchases with their values. Beyond the act of paying, the real shift was in perception: the 'cheap' price was revealed as an illusion, sustained by the silent exploitation of ecosystems and workers.

Kellie, our head of regeneration, contacted True Price, and together with GIST Impact, a leading sustainability analytics firm that helps companies measure their real-world impacts, we began the process of assessing our own true costs through an IP&L (integrated profit and loss) framework. This expands accounting beyond financial profit to include four types of capital: natural (the health of ecosystems and resources we depend on), human (the wellbeing, skills and development of people), produced (the financial and physical assets a business creates) and social (the strength of communities and relationships).

Our IP&L assessment gave us, for the first time, a true multi-capital view of our business. It showed us not just the financials, but the full ripple effect of our business actions on people, planet and place. What it revealed was both sobering and galvanising.

In **Natural Capital**, our direct operations in London had a relatively small footprint, with most impact coming from greenhouse gas emissions (around three-quarters), followed by waste and water use. Thanks to strong recycling practices, we've already cut waste-related impacts by a third. But the real story was upstream. A rapid estimation of our eight key suppliers, particularly in furniture, paints and cotton, revealed that the vast majority of our natural capital impacts come from this part of the chain, with air pollution from manufacturing and textiles being the most significant contributor. This confirmed what we suspected: if we want to meet our regenerative ambitions, supplier-level change is where we need to act first.

To kick off the True Cost review, we decided to go deep with the analysis of our two biggest product categories, fabric and wallpaper, which together make up 80 per cent of our business. Even though wallpaper accounted for 70 per cent of the impact measured, the report found we should be paying only around £0.20 more per square metre to meet its true cost – not a dramatic increase in real terms. Fabric, even though it made up just 30 per cent of the mix, came from a cotton supply chain where the hidden costs were far higher. Here, the analysis showed we should be paying a substantially more additional £2.76 per square metre.

This gave us the hard data we needed. Even though our wood pulp was sourced from FSC-certified forests in northern Europe, it was clear that we still needed to reduce the impact of our wallpaper. Through actions such as developing a tree-free base paper made from agricultural waste, rather than cutting down trees, we saw how a material negative could be transformed into a net benefit. But the real and urgent challenge lay in our cotton. Cotton is the world's most widespread and profitable non-food crop, employing over 250 million people globally. Yet its monocultural farming and conventional production comes at a high cost, which is rarely paid for as it erodes soil health and biodiversity, consuming up to 20,000 litres of water per kilo, its heavy chemical usage polluting rivers and harming communities. Most is grown by smallholder farmers in developing countries, often for low wages and with little security.

Faced with this reality and the data from our IP&L, we committed to phasing out Better Cotton – the world's largest cotton sustainability initiative, which focuses on reducing pesticide use, improving water efficiency and supporting farmer livelihoods, but stops short of full regenerative practices – and switching to regeneratively farmed cotton by 2027. We also pledged by that same date to regenerate land equivalent to all the cotton farming we have historically used.

For wallpaper, our goals are equally ambitious: to make all designs forest-fibre free by 2030; to replant and protect by 2026 the equivalent number of trees we have used historically; and from that year onwards, to safeguard the equivalent area of forest land used in our production annually.

We couldn't be put off by the fact that regenerative cotton velvet or tree-free wallpaper didn't yet exist. Instead, it spurred us on to work with the paper and cotton industries to try to create them and to then share them with other interiors brands so that we can accelerate this path towards regeneration together.

As we progress on our journey, our goal is for these true costs to steadily fall, even if the financial cost of doing business rises due to the investments needed to improve our supply chain. A reduction of these ecological and societal costs will be proof that we are no longer just extracting value from people and Nature but restoring and regenerating it.

Our **Human Capital** value, measured in terms of wages, benefits, training, wellbeing and the overall positive impact on employees, came back with very strong results, at just over £2 million. The data revealed that House of Hackney created particular value for women, who make up the majority of our workforce, through fair pay, good working conditions and opportunities for growth. What struck me most was the value that is created simply by investing in our people – in their skills, their growth and their long-term earning potential. This data and value confirmed that skills, knowledge and creativity are not only present but growing and that investment in training is paying off in higher productivity, adaptability and resilience. When you nurture the people, you nurture the business itself and a strong human capital value means the company's greatest asset, its people, is thriving. It reflects a team capable of carrying the business forwards through change, and of generating long-term value that no building, machine or balance-sheet entry could ever match.

In **Produced Capital**, the insights were that most of the value we create flows outward to employees through wages, to suppliers through fair payments, to government through taxes and to partners through shared projects, rather than pooling at the bottom line with shareholder primacy. Factually, a strong produced capital position means the business is generating healthy added financial value and distributing it across its ecosystem, signalling operational efficiency, reliability and trustworthiness to those who depend on us. In practice, it's proof that profit is serving its purpose: the circulatory system of a living economy – fuelling livelihoods, services and collaboration, instead of being an end in itself.

Social Capital is the value created through relationships that flow between a business, its communities and the ecosystems it touches. It's a measure of trust, reciprocity and mutual benefits: how deeply we are connected to our communities and how those connections translate into tangible, positive change. In our case, one partnership with the World Land Trust really stood out. The social return of the programme was £1.84 of social and environmental value for every £1 invested, generated through forest restoration, carbon sequestration and the creation of local employment. To put that into perspective, every pound we invest is working almost twice as hard, not to generate financial profit for us, but to deliver measurable good for people and planet. In a world where most business investments are judged solely on monetary return to shareholders, this reframes the conversation entirely: the highest-performing investments may be the ones that restore, protect and regenerate life itself.

Seeing our capitals through this expanded lens made one thing unshakably clear: profit alone could never tell the full story. The health of our company is inseparable from the health of the living systems and communities we touch.

When a tree is felled for wallpaper, the value of the forest, the loss of habitat and even the absence of the butterfly becomes part of the financial story. These costs are not abstract. They are measurable and, through regeneration, repayable. At the heart of this work lies a simple but radical idea: the true cost of doing business belongs on the balance sheet. Every product begins with the land, the soil, the tree, the water, the pollinator. And yet, under traditional accounting, none of these living costs are recorded.

Importantly, this is not just a moral argument.

In the United Kingdom, HMRC (His Majesty's Revenue and Customs), the government authority responsible for collecting taxes, recognises that any cost incurred 'wholly and exclusively for the purposes of trade' qualifies as legitimate business expenditure under Section 34 of the Income Tax (Trading and Other Income) Act 2005. This means such costs can be recognised within a company's accounts. In other words, investing in the natural systems that sustain your trade – the forests, soils and biodiversity that make business possible – is not just an act of charity but should be a legitimate and necessary business cost. One that, in every sense, belongs on the balance sheet of the future.

For companies across every industry, this principle needs to translate into recognising restoration and regeneration projects as essential business investments – vital to maintaining the natural systems on which their supply chains depend. However, the current system still stops at a company's immediate environmental footprint, measuring only the direct impacts of its own operations, such as energy use and emissions, while ignoring the wider ecological repair needed to sustain the landscapes and ecosystems that make production possible in the first place. For small and medium-sized enterprises, the gap is even wider: they are not required to report on their environmental footprint at all, nor is there a mechanism within accounting or tax systems to recognise the value of their regenerative investments.

The new business model we are developing, and the Nature-centric profit and loss accounting within it, is designed to change that. Working alongside economists and business leaders, our aim is to bring the invisible back into view by linking materials directly to their ecological impacts. Designed to be both credible and accessible, we want to open-source this framework through a 'greenprint' that will launch in 2027: a practical tool to help SMEs measure their true impact, make regenerative decisions with the same rigour applied to financial performance and help shift the culture of business at large. As part of the greenprint, we are working within existing systems to have Nature-based costs formally recognised as legitimate business expenditure, collaborating with auditors and accountants to build the audit trails and accounting standards that could enable every company, especially SMEs, to measure, report and take responsibility for their true impact.

This connects directly to the idea of 'going concern', the statement that determines whether a company is robust enough to continue trading into the future. Until now, this has referred only to financial sustainability. But a business cannot be truly viable if the ecosystems it depends on are collapsing. If the forests fall, if the soils degrade, if the waters are poisoned – we sabotage not just our ecosystems but the very ground our businesses stand on. By integrating this truth into the audit process, we have the potential to redefine what it means for a business to be sustainable: that the health of Nature is not external to our balance sheet but the foundation of it.

Imagine a world where restoring land and protecting biodiversity are not acts of charity but standard business practice; where regeneration is rewarded, not penalised; and where profit and planet are no longer seen as opposites but as part of the same living system. The task at hand is to bring this world forwards – and we are already beginning to live it into being.

The butterfly, the forest and the soil will no longer be silent partners in our business success but will be recognised as true stakeholders in value creation. By bringing their wellbeing into our accounting and governance, we begin to restore balance not only in our books but in the world of which we are a part. In this new model, profit still matters – but as a means, not the end. As the fuel that supports livelihoods, restores ecosystems, uplifts communities, invests in creativity and stewards resources for future generations. Profit becomes the oxygen that keeps the work alive, but it is no longer the fire itself.

Our framework will set holistic targets across financial vitality, planetary health, social and cultural wellbeing, organisational resilience and long-term legacy. Some will be measurable, others will need to be felt through the signs of increased aliveness and mutual flourishing. More importantly, they will be lived and held with humility – because the questions we ask of ourselves are often as important as the numbers we report.

In 2026, as part of our year-end, we will lodge our social and environmental costs of goods sold alongside our financial results at Companies House – the UK's official public register for company accounts. By doing so, we are making a public commitment to treat them as vital indicators of performance and not as invisible externalities to be ignored or deferred. If we are serious about redefining success, it must show up not only in our strategy but also in our reporting. That means publishing our financial profit and loss as well as our ecological, human and social balance sheets: the numbers that speak to the health we have created, the harm we have reduced and the living systems we have helped restore. True accountability means putting our values on the public record. This is how we begin to redefine what 'value' means in business – and who gets to count. Because if SMEs, the life force of our economies, start counting what truly counts, we can shift the future of business from the ground up.

But there is another system that must evolve alongside business itself: investment finance. Capital is the lifeblood that keeps enterprise alive. It determines what grows and what withers, who gets to scale and who is left behind. Just as businesses need to transform their relationship with Nature, investors, banks and governments must transform their relationship with money.

If capital continues to flow towards narrow, short-term gain, regenerative businesses – even those businesses with purpose at their cores – will struggle to thrive. Right now, the financial system is still pricing risk through an outdated lens, and if it doesn't evolve it will become a bottleneck to the transformation we urgently need. Just as we are reimagining our relationship with Nature, we must also reimagine our relationship with money: as a resource that flows to enable the regeneration of the whole.

We need investors who value a company for its margins as well as for its contribution to life, who understand that long-term resilience doesn't always show up in a spreadsheet but in a company's culture, its care for people and its impact on place. We need banks willing to underwrite the future, not just the past, and to lend based on holistic business health, not only EBITDA. And just as regenerative farmers receive incentives for restoring soil, we need governments to incentivise and reward regenerative businesses in order to accelerate it – through tax reform, grants, procurement policies and levies that make life-positive enterprise the norm and not the exception.

When we stop seeing Nature as separate from us and remember that we are part of Her, everything shifts. We awaken to the beauty of life, to the miracle of being here at all, and begin to value it as our most precious inheritance. Business stops being extractive and becomes relational. Work becomes purposeful and sacred again. Profit becomes one outcome of a system rooted in care and not just the goal itself.

Leaving a legacy is not about leaving money in the bank; it is about leaving the world more alive, more beautiful and more whole than we found it.

That is the true balance sheet of life.

Motherland

'Another world is not only possible, she's on her way. ... On a quiet day, if I listen very carefully, I can hear her breathing.'

Arundhati Roy, *War Talk*

The timing was not quite what I had planned but it just so happened that this book began on 6 November 2024, the day the US election results broke. The night before, like so many of us, I had gone to bed restless, carrying the collective unease of a world on edge, knowing that history was about to pivot, one way or another.

I somehow drifted into one of the most profound dreams that I can remember: the rare kind where your body truly unclenches and your soul sleeps like the dead. In it, I am sleeping high inside the creviced hollow of the great holm oak at Trematon, one of a pair of giant 600-year-old trees that stand like sentinels at the foot of the Norman motte, their wisdom and eldership holding court over the estate.

Inside the hollow is a cast-iron bed, perfectly encased by the tree trunk. I notice fronds of leaf motifs on the walls where there would normally be the imprints of the inner trunk's bark. The leaves look familiar to me and slowly I realise that the whole 'room' is wrapped in our Arborea tree-print wallpaper. It's a tapestry of painterly branches and leaves that swathe the entire tree-trunk room, including the ciderdown that I am tucked under and the pillow under my head, as it camouflages seamlessly with the living branches of the tree itself.

As I lie there, I feel utterly serene, secure, held – as if the great tree is cosseting me. I recognise it as the same feeling as being cradled in my mother's arms, or perhaps it's the deep sanctuary of the womb itself. In the dream, I know with certainty that the tree is Mother. Not just a metaphor, but Mother herself: sentient, nurturing, protective, eternal. Holding me in this first sanctuary of life, before separation.

Sleep held me through the night. Each time the urge rose to check the election results, the dream returned me to the tree-house bed, to the tree's embrace, determined to linger in its bliss for a little more. In my dream state, I knew with certainty that this was home – belonging, familial, safe.

Daylight pulled me harshly from that state, the feelings of connection abruptly replaced by the shock of the news and the stark reminder of a world unravelling in division.

I didn't try to decipher it at first, but subconsciously I think the Mother Tree dream arriving when it did, and staying so close, was no accident. It came as I was about to document the story that we were beginning to live, a story of interdependence and connection that stood in complete opposition to these new prevailing political winds. Winds that travelled quickly, dismantling hard-won progress on climate, diversity, equity and care. Winds that carried the icy breath of regression and separation.

Given the mood of futility and fragility, and the pace of global companies all too quick to seize on the rollbacks, it would have been easy to falter, to abandon the mission, to believe the tide was too strong and our work too small to matter. When we most needed to move forwards, the world seemed to lurch backwards.

When I needed the courage and resolve to keep going, I think the Mother Tree was showing me that beneath the turbulence of human systems there is a steadier ground. That home is not the outcome of elections or the rise and fall of empires, but the unconditional embrace of the Earth itself. And no matter how violently the structures of patriarchy grasp power, there is another way of being that is always available to us, rooted in nurture, mutuality and care. A mothering that does not dominate but steadies, protects and makes space for life to flourish.

This was, I see now, the subconscious reminder I most needed before beginning to write this book – that the deeper truth of our existence and our unique purpose is to return Home as participants and co-creators in Her living community. Beyond the short tenure of a political party, or a three-to-five-year business plan, our relationship with Nature, our true home, is untouchable, impenetrable and always available. It was also a reminder of the mothering needed right now in the form of stewardship – to help guide our adolescent species through its turbulence into a more mature relationship with life, where responsibility, reciprocity and reverence take the place of recklessness and extraction. For I have come to see that motherhood is not just about raising a child, but a way of being in relationship with life itself. It is the instinct to protect, regenerate and create the conditions in which life can truly flourish.

Somehow my fire stayed lit, anchoring me in the belief that we do not need to be lost; that the memory of our place in Nature still lives on innately in our very cells if we only tap into it; that Nature still holds the greenprint for how to live, and how to work, if we dare to put our phones down to watch and listen.

And perhaps our purpose as humans is not to strive for something, but to use our uniquely human gifts for something: our sensitivity that allows us to feel the pulse of the world, our intuition that guides us where logic doesn't always, our imagination that dreams new possibilities into being, our empathy that binds us to one another, our creativity that transforms vision into form, our foresight that lets us think generations ahead, and our storytelling that weaves meaning and belonging. In Japan, they call it *ikigai* - the perfect intersection where purpose is woven from what we love, what we are good at and what the world is asking of us. These gifts are not accidents – they are the very tools we need to become conscious participants in life's unfolding, to step into our true role as custodians and co-creators of the living world.

We are shaping House of Hackney in many ways to be the very opposite of the rollbacks and regressions that define this political chapter. Where corporations abandon their climate pledges, we are drawing closer and closer to Nature. Where others double down on short-term extraction, we are modelling long-term restoration. Where companies borrow Nature's names to market their wares, we are building a company in Her name, recognising Nature not as a backdrop to business but as a stakeholder, a relation, a community, an ecosystem to which we belong.

We remember that our people – present and future – are biological beings born of Nature, reflecting Her inherent diversity of species, identities and genders. As the corporate world regresses, we step forwards into the work of imagining and embodying the future we long for. And like Nature, House of Hackney needs to be a home for everyone.

But these transitional times, though uncertain, can also be fertile ground. What feels like unpredictability can also be seen as a world of possibility. There's no sign in the dead of winter that the world will be reborn, and yet spring arrives in all its vitality, almost shockingly, every year. And even in those depths of winter, when the surface seems barren, the unseen rooting is happening underground. It is this deep work, this work that is happening on the periphery in our communities, in our fields, in our companies. This is *radical* work in the truest sense of the word – from the Latin *radix*, meaning 'root'. Go beneath the surface and this transformation is already underway as it quietly creates the conditions so that new life can break through.

In the books I read, the story of separation – the history we have lived through – is often followed by the story of *interbeing*: a future in which we remember our place as conscious participants in the ecosystems of life, within our shared home of Nature. This is the story we now have the opportunity, and the duty, to create as we return to our roots before it is too late. And though the roots remain underground and mostly unseen, some are starting to peek through as shoots of life and hope. And action is always shaped by vision. How we see the world has everything to do with what we can do in the world. And contrary to what we are made to believe in this moment, we *do* have agency to change the story, but dismantling the narratives that trap us is foundational to creating the new realities we need.

Change often begins in the periphery, rooted in the underground, with movements and thinkers who are often dismissed as insignificant.

Rosa Parks on that bus that day would not have known that her refusal would ripple into a global civil rights movement. Few expected the Berlin Wall to fall until it did – and almost overnight – catalysed by ordinary people who gathered and refused the old order.

What starts as a shift in consciousness, or a new story, can become law, policy and cultural change. History shows us it does not take a majority to change the world. Small acts at the margins often become the seeds of change. Political scientist Erica Chenoweth, analysing over a century of resistance movements worldwide, found that transformative change has never required a majority. In fact, history shows us that nonviolent movements that mobilise and sustain active participation from around 3.5 per cent of a population consistently succeeded in achieving their aims. Small, committed minorities can catalyse some serious systemic change. Which means that if even a small fraction of businesses chooses to act regeneratively, it could be enough to tip the scales towards a life-sustaining economy.

This echoes the power of the SME community: small, mighty and entrepreneurial. Though each may seem small in scale, let's remember that together SMEs make up 99 per cent of all private sector businesses – a collective far beyond the threshold for transformation. In a world that can feel beholden to big corporations, big government and big finance, SMEs remind us that we do, in fact, have agency. More than that – we have both the opportunity and the responsibility to chart a new way.

When we align our businesses with Nature, we are capable of profound influence far beyond our sectors. SMEs sit close to community, culture and creativity. If we use our agency with intention – if we return to the original root of 'company', where we metaphorically share bread together – we can reshape supply chains and model new economies where the flourishing of life is the measure of success.

This is a journey with no final destination. It is not a place we can arrive at or a line we can cross once and for all. But it is a practice – a way of being in relationship with life, in the company of Nature that leaves us feeling at our most *alive*. For me, for our company, and for all who are willing, this journey is about moving ever deeper into connection with Nature inner and outer.

My story, is your story, is our story.

We are the bridge generation. Standing between the story of separation and the underground work needed to root the story of interbeing. But bridges are not endpoints – they are built to be crossed.

And our purpose is to hold steady, to carry others across to this new reality of companies and communities rooted in life.

To be the bridge that we travel across to make our way home.

The future is shaped by what we do in the present.

And the present is alive in our hands.

ACKNOWLEDGEMENTS

With gratitude…

This book could not have been written without the strong foundation I have been given in life – for which I am profoundly grateful.

To my parents and my sister, Laura – thank you for giving me the bedrock of safety from which to leap and the freedom to dream big without fear of consequence. It is the greatest gift a child could receive.

To my husband, Javvy. Meeting you opened the channel through which these ideas could take root. The way you see the awe and beauty of the world and its inhabitants is a constant, humble reminder for me to do the same. Walking this path with you is the greatest privilege of my life.

To Javi and Lila, our children and our teachers – you are both the mirror and the compass, guiding us to make the world more beautiful for you and for all future generations. The sensitivity and empathy in your generation give me hope beyond words and must surely be part of Nature's evolution. We owe it to you, and to those who come after you, to leave our world better than we found it.

To our House of Hackney family – our beloved team, suppliers and factories – thank you for building the house and planting the garden with us. Your imagination and resilience hold me every day. We could not ask for a better leader than Sam Dent – thank you for innately knowing what truly matters in running a company.

I am deeply grateful to Chelsea Green Publishing for believing in this journey. To Charles Miers, who first heard me speak at the Real Farming Conference in Oxford – thank you for backing a new writer with a wild vision for business to be in service to life. To my editors, Muna and Susan – thank you for your gentle and skilful hands in shaping the manuscript, for allowing my voice to remain my own and for your patience and understanding that I was both simultaneously living the book and writing the book, and that a living breathing organisation does not stand still.

To Kellie Dalton, Brontie Ansell, Charmian Love and Jessie Mond Wedd – thank you for your courage and intuitive wisdom in helping us rethink business in these times, and for walking with us as we find the way together.

To Simeon Rose and Anne Hopkins of Faith in Nature – for dreaming into being a world in which Mother Nature has a voice within our companies, and for having the courage to make it real. You were the architects of a paradigm we didn't yet have language for, but instinctively knew we were missing – one that fundamentally changed how we experience the world and conduct our company.

And to Lawyers for Nature, for translating that vision into law, and for helping build the legal architecture that allowed Nature to truly take a seat at the table.

To my teachers, many of whom live in these pages – the writers who understand the power of a book to change how we see the world. May the seeds of your ideas continue to be planted, tended and to grow.

And finally, to Mother Nature – my greatest teacher. Sitting outside and writing through the turning of the seasons, these words often felt less mine than Hers.

This book is, ultimately, an offering back to Her – the muse, the mentor and the home to which we all belong.

The Voice of Mother Nature and Future Generations' Reply

In Response to House of Hackney's 'Impact Report 2025'

The voice of Mother Nature and Future Generations has been given time and space to reply to this report compiled by the staff and directors of House of Hackney Limited. The reply was written by the holder of the board position during the time period this report covers, the financial year 2024–25, from 6 April 2024 to 5 April 2025. The contents of the reply were not influenced by any other director or member of staff. This reply was also not edited by the House of Hackney leadership team prior to publication.

Mother Nature & Voices of
Future Generations' Reply 2024–25

Under the stewardship of lawyers from Lawyers for Nature, House of Hackney took the bold and imaginative step of granting Mother Nature and the voices of Future Generations their respective seats at the board-room table. This decision is more than symbolic; it represents a profound structural shift in corporate governance, one that acknowledges the natural world, and those yet to be born, as rightful participants in shaping the future of business. In so doing, House of Hackney has aligned itself with a growing movement that recognises the Rights of Nature now and the responsibilities we owe to those who will inherit the consequences of our present actions.

Over the past year, this governance shift has translated into a range of substantive actions and achievements. There is much to be celebrated. The company has continued to embed ecological awareness into its core operations and creative practice. Designs that draw inspiration from Nature have been matched by tangible measures to respect and regenerate it. The work that the team have been doing on engagement with regenerative cotton and other materials, research into zero fossil fuel paint and wood fibre-free wallpaper alternatives demonstrates a willingness to innovate way beyond standard supply chain management. Their efforts start with the acknowledgement that beauty in design cannot be detached from the ecological realities of extraction and manufacture.

Material innovation has also expanded to include mycelium and cork, offering new possibilities for products that can be entirely composted back to the earth with no trace. These developments are significant not only for their environmental benefits, but also for the cultural message they carry: that luxury and responsibility can coexist, and that design can be both visionary and restorative.

Despite its modest size the company has made a formidable effort to understand and address its part in the urgent challenges of deforestation and biodiversity loss. Through its partnership with the World Land Trust, House of Hackney has directly contributed to the protection of endangered woodland. This commitment is more than compensatory; it represents restitution, recognising that a business drawing upon the stories of Nature and her work must also work to contribute to its survival and restoration.

Alongside these ecological measures, important progress has been made in accounting for the genuine impact on the one and only home humans have (and of course, share, with so many others). Work on the company's carbon footprint has been undertaken and this will be redone again in 2026, focussing on the reduction of Scope 3 supply chain emissions with suppliers. This work is vital, as it opens the door to more accurate reporting and credible reduction strategies in the years ahead.

Coupled with this has been the adoption of a 'True Cost' framework. This was a phenomenal piece of work that is market leading and one the company should be incredibly proud of starting. It is not an easy conversation to have in a profit driven environment. Nonetheless, this is a company who is prepared to issue a significant challenge to the current societal notions of business success. By recognising social and ecological impacts as part of the company's ledger, House of Hackney is beginning to model what a regenerative economy in service of life might truly look like in the centuries ahead.

Community and advocacy work have also been central to this year's activities. The pledge to donate 1% of all sales to environmental and social causes has given tangible weight to the company's commitments, while initiatives such as The Garden of Tomorrow festival and the We Are Nature campaign have extended these commitments into the cultural sphere. These projects are notable not only for their reach but for their ethos: they re-position the work of design as a cultural act with ecological and ethical consequences. Partnerships with organisations such as Stop Ecocide International further demonstrate a willingness to use the company's platform for advocacy, seeking systemic change beyond its own operations. It is of course also worth noting that there is now a conspicuous absence of partnerships with those entities who, for whatever reason, do not share the same ethics as House of Hackney. Grace and hope is sometimes also found in those things which we choose not to do.

Taken as a whole, these actions reflect a shift in both culture and practice. They show that ecological responsibility is not an adjunct to business but can be at its very heart. It is not simply a 'nice to have' or a regularly forgotten KPI on the ESG register. These people also show others that creativity and responsibility are not opposing forces but interwoven strands of the same fabric.

Yet the challenges ahead are significant and it must be recognised that this work is only just beginning. Supply chains remain complex, and true accountability to the land, waters, and communities that provide raw materials must deepen further. The collection of the accurate data must continue apace, despite the costs in time and effort. For without this true accounting business consciously chooses to remain ignorant. The minimisation of waste, reduction of energy use, and broadening the accessibility of regenerative design are areas that require sustained attention. As with the artistry of the company's patterns, the work of guardianship is never finished; it is an evolving canvas, demanding humility, curiosity, and persistence.

What distinguishes House of Hackney is its cultural influence. The company is more than a designer and producer of interiors: it is a storyteller, shaping the ways in which people imagine their homes and, by extension, their place in the wider world. To place Mother Nature and Voices of Future Generations at the centre of this storytelling is to acknowledge that design is not neutral. It can obscure ecological realities, or it can illuminate the truth of interdependence and shared belonging. House of Hackney has begun to demonstrate, with care and time, that the latter is possible. Their work shows that business can re-enchant rather than exploit, that beauty can serve as a form of justice, and that design can carry within it a duty of care.

This year has shown a business that can be bold, creative, and commercially successful while honouring ecological responsibility. The company has laid important foundations for a model of regenerative business that blends imagination with accountability. The journey ahead is long, but the path is clear. With continued persistence, innovation, and care, House of Hackney can continue to model how culture, responsibility and business might be rewoven into a pattern with the enduring voice of Mother Nature and the needs of Future Generations at its heart.

Mother Nature & Voices of Future Generations
April 2025

As represented by the then guardian, Brontie Ansell.

FIELD NOTES

The following works and platforms have helped shape the worldview behind this book. They are not simply texts to read but companions for practice – invitations to think differently, lead differently and remember our place within our awe-inspiring living world.

Further Reading

Abram, David. *The Spell of the Sensuous*. Vintage, 1997. Reawakens the senses and reminds us that Earth is a living, communicative presence.

Beresford-Kroeger, Diana. *To Speak for the Trees*. Timber Press, 2021. A scientist-storyteller's call to protect forests as living elders.

Berry, Thomas. *The Great Work*. Crown, 2000. Names our historical moment as the transition to an Earth-centred civilisation.

Chouinard, Yvon. *Let My People Go Surfing*. Penguin, 2016. An unconventional business memoir arguing that companies can serve the planet first and profit as a consequence.

Cullinan, Cormac. *Wild Law*. Green Books, 2011. Advocates for legal systems that recognise the rights of the Earth community.

Davidson, Jane. *#futuregen*. Chelsea Green Publishing, 2020. A practical account of embedding future generations into law and governance.

Fullerton, John B. *Regenerative Economics*. New Society Publishers, 2026. Offers living-systems principles as a blueprint for redesigning economics and finance.

Hopkins, Rob. *How to Fall in Love with the Future*. Chelsea Green Publishing, 2025. A hopeful call to reclaim imagination as a practical force for shaping regenerative futures.

Hundley, Jessica, ed. *Library of Esoterica*. 6 vols. Taschen, 2020–2025. A visual archive of myth and symbolism that nourishes cultural imagination.

Ichioka, Sarah and Michael Pawlyn. *Flourish*. Triarchy Press, 2021. A call to move beyond sustainability towards regenerative design for long-term flourishing.

Kimmerer, Robin Wall. *Braiding Sweetgrass*. Penguin, 2020. Restores reciprocity and gratitude as the foundation of right relationship with the more-than-human world.

Krznaric, Roman. *The Good Ancestor*. W.H. Allen, 2021. An invitation to expand our time horizons in service of future generations.

Kumar, Satish. *Radical Love*. Parallax Press, 2023. A reminder that love must sit at the heart of transformation.

Louv, Richard. *Last Child in the Woods*. Atlantic Books, 2010. A seminal exploration of 'nature-deficit disorder' and the importance of direct contact with the natural world.

Macfarlane, Robert. *Is a River Alive?* Penguin, 2026. Explores the movement to recognise rivers and ecosystems as living entities with legal standing and a voice.

Marquis, Christopher. *The Profiteers*. PublicAffairs, 2024. Examines the gap between corporate sustainability rhetoric and structural reform.

Marvel, Kate. *Human Nature*. Scribe, 2025. A deeply humane reflection on grief, courage and responsibility in the climate era.

Meadows, Donella H., Denis L. Meadows, Jørgen Randers and William W. Behrens III. *The Limits to Growth*. Universe Books, 1972. A landmark systems study demonstrating the risks of exponential growth on a finite planet.

Miles, Ellen, ed. *Nature Is a Human Right*. DK, 2022. Argues that access to Nature is essential to dignity, wellbeing and justice.

Oliver, Mary. *Devotions*. Corsair, 2023. Luminous poetry that restores reverence for the ordinary wild.

Raworth, Kate. *Doughnut Economics*. Cornerstone, 2018. Reimagines economic success as thriving within planetary boundaries.

Rose, Simeon. *Nature's Boardroom*. Bristol University Press, 2026. Explores how corporate governance can formally embed Nature into decision-making.

Schumacher, E.F. *Small Is Beautiful*. Vintage, 1993. A prophetic call for human-scale, values-led enterprise.

Seligman, Martin. *Flourish*. John Murray Press, 2011. Introduces the science of positive psychology, reframing success as human flourishing.

Solnit, Rebecca. *No Straight Road Takes You There*. Granta Books, 2025. Essays on climate, justice and the nonlinear pathways of change.

Suzuki, David. *The Sacred Balance*. Greystone Books, 2007. Explores the profound interdependence between planetary health and human wellbeing.

Wahl, Daniel Christian. *Designing Regenerative Cultures.* Triarchy Press, 2016. A systems-thinking roadmap for organisations seeking to operate in alignment with life.

Organisations and Platforms

Atmos (https://atmos.earth) A cultural platform exploring the intersection of climate, creativity and ecological imagination.

B Lab (https://www.bcorporation.net/en-us) A global movement certifying and supporting businesses committed to stakeholder governance and purpose beyond profit.

Biomimicry Institute (https://www.biomimicry.org) Advancing innovation inspired by Nature's 3.7 billion years of research and development.

Bioneers (https://bioneers.org) Convening innovators and visionaries working at the frontiers of ecological and social regeneration.

Capital Institute (https://capitalinstitute.org) Advancing regenerative economic theory and practice grounded in living-systems principles.

Deep Time Walk (https://www.deeptimewalk.org) An experiential learning journey through Earth's 4.6-billion-year history that cultivates awe and planetary perspective.

Doughnut Economics Action Lab (https://doughnuteconomics.org) Providing tools and case studies to help cities, governments and businesses operate within planetary boundaries.

Earth Law Center (https://www.earthlawcenter.org) Advancing legal frameworks that recognise ecosystems as living entities with inherent rights.

Earthed (https://www.earthed.co) An online learning platform offering accessible courses and conversations to support ecological literacy and regeneration.

Global Alliance for the Rights of Nature (https://www.garn.org) A global movement promoting Earth-centred jurisprudence and the recognition of Nature's legal rights.

Lawyers for Nature (https://www.lawyersfornature.com) Supporting legal innovation that embeds the rights of Nature within governance and corporate structures.

nRhythm (https://www.nrhythm.co) Helping organisations align strategy and culture with natural cycles and regenerative rhythms.

Resurgence Trust (https://www.resurgence.org) A long-standing voice for ecological philosophy and regenerative culture.

Wellbeing Economy Alliance (https://weall.org) A global alliance working to redesign economic systems around human and ecological wellbeing.

INDEX

ABOUT THE AUTHOR

Frieda Gormley is the co-founder of House of Hackney, the British B Corp interiors brand that is redefining what business can be when it works in partnership with Nature. Born in Ireland, her early years were shaped by creativity, curiosity and a back garden that was her endless universe. Inspired by her grandmother's love of antiques and textiles, Frieda developed a deep appreciation for heritage and craftsmanship. Alongside her creative instincts, her entrepreneurial talent surfaced early  and she was named Young Entrepreneur of Ireland at just thirteen.

Frieda began her career in fashion buying at Dunnes Stores, Ireland's largest retailer, where international sourcing trips exposed her to the exploitation inherent in high-street production. In 2004, she joined Topshop in London under the mentorship of Jane Shepherdson, who first showed her that business could be a force for good. Confronted with the environmental toll of fast fashion and the deeper question of legacy after becoming a mother, Frieda felt called to root her work and life in a more meaningful relationship with the living world.

While seeking interiors for their new home that were beautiful, responsibly made and inspired by Nature, Frieda and her husband, Javvy M. Royle, identified a gap in the market. They founded House of Hackney in 2011 as an alternative to disposable design: a brand grounded in British craftsmanship, creativity and community with Nature as design muse.

A pivotal shift came in 2019, when they became custodians of a Cornish castle and its nine acres of wild gardens. Immersed in the landscape and guided by regenerative-farmer neighbours, Frieda experienced what she calls *a remembering* as she began to understand Nature not only as inspirer but as teacher and strategic guide, with Her 3.7-billion-year evolutionary wisdom offering a greenprint for how companies can thrive.

This awakening led House of Hackney to become only the second company in the world to legally appoint Mother Nature to its board, integrating ecological and long-term stakeholder considerations into governance, supply base, culture and even the balance sheet.

Today, House of Hackney is recognised as a pioneering model for regenerative business, showing how creativity, profitability and positive impact can coexist. Frieda is an emerging voice in the movement, advocating for enterprises that honour creativity, community and the living world. Her work, and this book, reflects her belief that business can be a vessel for healing, imagination and the flourishing of all life.